FRESH MEXICAN

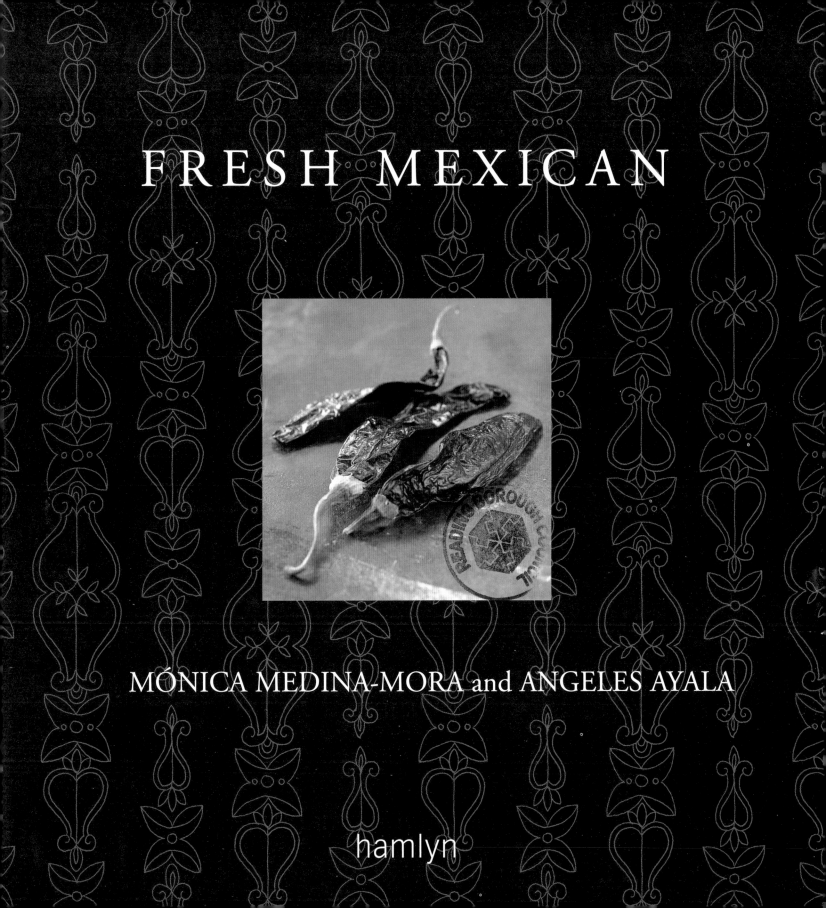

MÓNICA MEDINA-MORA and ANGELES AYALA

hamlyn

Note

Both metric and imperial measurements have been given in all recipes.

Use one set of measurements only, and not a mixture of both.

Standard level spoon measurements are used in all recipes.

1 tablespoon = one 15 ml spoon

1 teaspoon = one 5 ml spoon

The Department of Health advises that eggs should not be consumed raw. This book contains some dishes made with raw or lightly cooked eggs. It is prudent for vulnerable people such as pregnant and nursing mothers, invalids, the elderly, babies and young children to avoid uncooked or lightly cooked dishes made with eggs. Once prepared, these dishes should be kept refrigerated and used promptly.

This book includes dishes made with nuts and nut derivatives. It is advisable for those with known allergic reactions to nuts and nut derivatives and those who may be potentially vulnerable to these allergies, such as pregnant and nursing mothers, invalids, the elderly, babies and children to avoid dishes made with nuts and nut oils. It is also prudent to check the labels of pre-prepared ingredients for the possible inclusion of nut derivatives.

Ovens should be preheated to the specified temperature – if using a fan-assisted oven, follow the manufacturer's instructions for adjusting the time and the temperature.

Fresh herbs should be used unless otherwise stated.

Medium eggs should be used unless otherwise stated.

An Hachette Livre UK Company

First published in Great Britain in 2007 by
Hamlyn, a division of Octopus Publishing Group Ltd
2–4 Heron Quays, London E14 4JP

ISBN-13: 978-0-600-61683-2
ISBN-10: 0-600-61683-5

A CIP catalogue record for this book is available from the British Library

Printed and bound in China

10 9 8 7 6 5 4 3 2 1

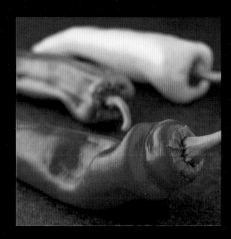

Contents

Introduction

Be prepared for a really unforgettable assault on your senses, for authentic Mexican cooking offers one of the most exciting culinary experiences in the world. Explosions of colour, captivating aromas, deliciously rich flavours and stunning textures combine to produce a distinctive and truly great celebration of food. The range of dishes, ingredients and regional specialities to be savoured reflect the vibrant culture of Mexico and its origins in the pre-Hispanic world.

Essential ingredients

Mexican cuisine benefits from its reliance on fresh ingredients. The land of many different types of chilli, Mexico has long been the provider of important ingredients for the Old World: corn, an essential staple and regarded as a sacred food by the Native Americans, vanilla pods, avocados, tomatoes and the revered cacao bean – the essential ingredient for chocolate – which at one time served as currency among the native traders. The arrival of the Spanish Conquistadores in the 16th century enriched and enhanced the national menu by introducing their own preferred ingredients, such as pork, beef, lamb, chicken, chickpeas, cabbages, sugar cane and citrus fruits. Over time, a fusion of the two cultures took place and culminated in a unique cuisine that boasts a stunning range of dishes, as you will discover from the selection in this book.

Mexican fare can claim its place as one of the forefathers of the global kitchen, having introduced the world to many of the ingredients used in its daily cooking. How would Mediterranean dishes manage without tomatoes? As for the prospect of dessert menus deprived of chocolate, it simply doesn't bear thinking about! And try to imagine how different some of your favourite dishes from South-East Asian cuisines would taste without the distinctive heat and piquancy that chilli brings to them.

Enriched by regionality

Regional variation in cooking techniques, ingredients and flavourings is one of the key factors that makes Mexican cooking such an exciting cuisine. The country has defined regional boundaries, creating self-contained communities that use locally grown ingredients with local cooking techniques and finishing touches for many of the national dishes.

Healthy traditions

A lesser-known contribution that Mexican cuisine brings to the global kitchen is a wide choice of wholesome and nutritious meals, prepared with healthy cooking methods and the right combination of ingredients to guarantee balanced meal plans. Many dishes are still prepared in the same healthy ways that were once practised before the arrival of the Spanish. Steaming, poaching and boiling are some of the most common methods used, and nothing is thrown away, so cooking liquids and the valuable nutrients they contain are incorporated in the dishes. Another plus point is that sauces are very healthy, as they are commonly thickened either by reduction or with ground seeds or maize, without the addition of butter or cream. This is why Mexican cookery fits so well with the modern-day focus on the pursuit of physical wellbeing and healthy eating.

Cook, eat and enjoy!

Mexican cuisine cannot fail to captivate your taste buds, entertain your guests and broaden your culinary know-how. Enjoy the discovery of new ingredients and new methods, and savour the experience of Mexican cooking!

Eating the Mexican way

For the full, authentic experience of eating *a la mexicana*, a whistlestop guide through the country's daily eating habits helps to set the scene for Mexican cookery and puts the dishes that are described in the book in context.

The big breakfast

The working day in Mexico either starts very early in the morning with a light breakfast of coffee and a sweet roll, or slightly later with a full-blown *desayuno*.

This wholesome and nutritional breakfast begins with a plate of fresh seasonal fruit and a glass of fruit juice. The bold array of colours from the oranges, strawberries, limes, golden mangoes and papayas makes an effective wake-up call by itself.

The next course is a plate of eggs, cooked in a variety of different ways and accompanied by beans and a chilli sauce, which is guaranteed to liven up your taste buds. This dish is usually eaten with warm tortillas (the traditional flattened corn bread) or a crusty *bolillo* (petit pain) and beans. A selection of sweet rolls, coffee and hot chocolate rounds off the breakfast perfectly. This style of breakfast provides a great start to the day.

Late lunch

As the main meal of the day rarely starts before two o'clock in the afternoon, the benefits of a proper breakfast are fully appreciated by Mexicans. *La comida* (lunch) observes a time-honoured formula. The opening course of soup is always followed by a plate of rice, which is treated as a separate serving. Next, there is a main dish of meat or fish, accompanied by vegetables and salad, with beans available as an optional extra. Chilli sauce and warm tortillas are on offer throughout the meal. The lunch experience is rounded off with seasonal fruit or a dessert. *Aguas frescas* – fresh fruit beverages – are offered during the meal. They make perfect thirst-quenchers that can be enjoyed at any time of the day.

Light supper

Moving on to the evening, *la cena* (supper) tends to be a light meal served between eight or nine o'clock. Sometimes an *antojito* (snack) is prepared, or some of the lunchtime dishes are reheated. In summer, a crisp salad or fresh fruit medley is sufficient.

Sustaining and special snacks

Especially at weekends or on special occasions, *botanas* (appetizers) are served before a main meal, usually accompanied by a drink. Typical *botanas* include guacamole, fresh cheese, pickled vegetables and a variety of *antojitos*, such as *tacos*, *quesadillas* and *tostadas*. *Antojitos* are also perfect when you need to tide over hunger until the next meal and can be enjoyed 'on the go', bought from street vendors who offer an impressive range of snacks from their improvised stands. Whatever the time of day in Mexico, you can always be sure of finding something tasty and satisfying to eat!

The Mexican larder

The distinctive qualities of Mexican dishes are provided by a winning combination of flavoursome ingredients, including fresh and dried chillies – some hot and pungent, some mild and sweet; aromatic spices (cinnamon, cumin, cloves and black pepper); essential herbs such as *epazote*, coriander, oregano and thyme; sesame and pumpkin seeds, almonds and other nuts; juicy tomatoes, *tomatillos*, onions and garlic, sometimes roasted to deepen their flavours; tasty cheeses; and sharp limes and other citrus fruits that give zing and colour to a dish. In short, a multitude of healthy and nutritious vegetables, greens, grains, meats and a remarkable variety of fish and shellfish define the Mexican larder.

Below is a list of some of the main ingredients used in Mexican cooking and featured in the book. Most of them are available from standard supermarkets, while others, such as dried chillies, can be found in specialist and ethnic shops or purchased by mail order or from online suppliers.

AVOCADOS (AGUACATES) Avocados are widely used all over the country in sauces, *antojitos* (snacks), soups, salads, side dishes and main dishes. It is best to prepare them just before serving, as the flesh begins to darken soon after they are cut, although sprinkling them with lime juice helps to keep them green. Since avocados are rarely sold ripe, buy them a couple of days before they are needed. When ripe, they keep well for a few days in the refrigerator. Of the many varieties of avocado, the Hass avocado, with its knobbly black skin, is one of the most popular around the world. It ripens evenly, peels easily, keeps well and its flesh is full of flavour.

BEANS (FRIJOLES) Beans, rich in fibre and protein, together with chillies and maize are the staple foods of Mexico. They are important ingredients in many *antojitos*, and make delicious and nutritious soups, side dishes and main dishes. Freshly cooked beans can be kept for up to a week in the refrigerator and freeze very well. There are many different kinds of beans, varying in size and colour from dark black to nearly white. A popular variety is the small black bean, *frijol negro*, mainly used in the south of the country, the Gulf area and the Yucatan Peninsula. Other popular varieties are the *pinto*, the purplish coloured *flor the mayo* and the pale brown *bayo*, mainly used in central Mexico.

CHEESE (QUESO) There are good melting cheeses, such as *Oaxaca* and *Chihuahua*, used in *antojitos* and main dishes. These can be substituted with Gouda, mozzarella and mild Cheddar. *Queso fresco* is a fresh cheese with a slightly salty taste. It can be eaten by itself as a *botana* (appetizer), as well as cubed or crumbled over *antojitos*, salads, soups and main dishes. Greek feta cheese is a good substitute. *Queso panela*, a low-salt fresh cheese from central Mexico, is used in *antojitos* such as grilled cheese. An acceptable substitute is buffalo mozzarella.

CHILLIES (CHILES) Chillies provide many of the flavours, colours and textures that make Mexican dishes unique. They have an essential oil containing capsaicin, which is thought to be good for the heart and blood circulation and gives chillies their hot, piquant flavour. Chillies are available in Mexico in many different sizes, shapes and colours, fresh, dried, smoked or pickled.

Because of their heat, both fresh and dried chillies should be handled with care, preferably using rubber gloves. As a general rule, if you just want to add a very mild chilli flavour to a dish, add the whole chilli during cooking and discard it before serving. For a slightly hotter, more piquant flavour, cut the chillies in half lengthways, and remove any seeds and internal veins before adding to the dish. For a strong, full flavour, chop the chilli flesh, seeds and veins and add them all to the dish.

FRESH CHILLIES (CHILES FRESCOS) The following are a few of the most popular fresh chillies used frequently in Mexican cooking. *Habanero*, also known as Scotch bonnet, is used mainly in dishes from the Yucatan Peninsula, and is the hottest of all chillies. *Jalapeño*, named after Jalapa, the capital city of the state of Veracruz, is used extensively in salsas and cooked dishes, and is also ideal for pickling. *Poblano* is the largest chilli, and can be recognized by its dark green colour and pointed tip. It is always cooked before use, with its skin, seeds and veins removed. It is used extensively in soups and rice, meat and fish dishes. *Serrano* is a very popular, very hot, thin chilli and, like the *jalapeño*, is used in salsas, guacamole and cooked dishes.

DRIED CHILLIES (CHILES SECOS) A wide variety of dried chillies are available, each with its own distinctive flavour and colour. They are cooked with other ingredients to make chilli sauces and to flavour dishes. They are also used to make two classic Mexican sauces: *Adobo*, a seasoning sauce made with ground dried chillies, herbs and vinegar, and *Mole*, a cooked sauce made with mainly dried chillies, together with spices, seeds and sometimes a toasted corn tortilla, fruits or a piece of chocolate, all finely ground together. Chicken, meat or vegetable stock is also commonly used in its preparation. When buying dried chillies, look for ones that are firm and unbroken. *Ancho*, a dried *poblano* chilli with a dark wrinkly skin, is one of the most popular and mildest dried chilli. *Arbol*, a very hot chilli with a lovely red colour when dried, is used mainly in sauces and casseroles. *Chipotle* is a *jalapeño* that has been dried with warm smoke. It is available dried and either bottled or canned in an *adobo* sauce and gives food a distinctive smoky, slightly sweet flavour. *Guajillo* has an elegant burgundy-red colour. A sauce made with this chilli will have a rich colour and a medium-hot chilli flavour. *Mulato* is a dark skinned chilli with a medium-hot flavour. *Pasilla* is a long and narrow dried chilli with a dark brown colour, and its flavour varies from medium-hot to very hot. It is used extensively in *mole* sauces.

CHOCOLATE (CHOCOLATE) Chocolate is made from the seeds of the cacao tree. In Mexico, the cacao beans are ground with sugar and formed into tablets, to which cinnamon, almonds and vanilla are frequently added. This type of chocolate is used to make drinks and is sometimes added in small amounts to *mole* sauces.

CINNAMON (CANELA) This popular spice is obtained from the inner bark of the cinnamon tree. It is used in both savoury and sweet dishes.

FRESH CORIANDER (CILANTRO) This aromatic herb, rich in vitamin B, folic acid and essential oil, is widely used in Mexican dishes. It gives a distinctive flavour to salsas, soups, salads and main dishes. It is usually added chopped just before serving.

EPAZOTE This highly aromatic, strong-smelling herb is widely used in Mexico to flavour beans, soups, cooked vegetables and stews. Such is its unique flavour that no other herb can be used as a substitute for epazote. It is available dried from specialist Mexican food suppliers by mail order and online.

MAIZE (MAÍZ) Maize is a cereal that remains the main staple in the Mexican diet, and is used both dried and fresh. In the pre-Hispanic era, it was not only the main ingredient to feed the body, but also to feed the soul. In offerings to their gods, native Mexicans always included maize and objects made with it.

Dried maize (*Maíz*) is used to obtain *masa*, the dough from which corn tortillas are made. The dried maize kernels are briefly cooked with lime (calcium oxide) to remove their tough skins and make the cereal easy to digest and increase its nutritional value. The kernels are then ground to a paste, from which the *masa* is obtained. You can make *masa* using *masa harina* (not cornflour), found in many supermarkets, to make your own tortillas. Alternatively, you can buy them ready-made.

Fresh sweetcorn (*Elote*) is a favourite in Mexico. It has a delicate sweet flavour and is a good source of vitamins and

minerals. It is popular to eat it whole, as corn-on-the-cob, either boiled or roasted and seasoned with a half a lime, squeezed and spread over the corn and topped with chilli powder. Fresh corn cobs are frequently cut into pieces and added to casseroles. Fresh sweetcorn kernels are used in soups and vegetable dishes as well as cakes and breads. Nothing from the corn is left unused, as even the husks are used to wrap food for cooking.

NOPALES These are the fleshy oval tender leaves or paddles of the *nopal* cactus, and are very popular mainly in central Mexico. They are cooked and eaten in salads, soups, eggs dishes and stews. Bottled or canned nopales are an adequate substitute for fresh nopales, must be thoroughly rinsed before use. Nopales are available from specialist Mexican food shops and suppliers.

PUMPKIN SEEDS (PEPITAS) The seeds of various pumpkins and squashes were highly valued in Mexico long before the arrival of

the Spanish. They are eaten roasted and salted as a snack or used ground as a thickening agent in savoury dishes.

SESAME SEEDS (AJONJOLÍ) Widely cultivated in Mexico, sesame seeds have a nutty, slightly sweet flavour and are used toasted as a garnish for *mole* sauces and salads. They are also used as a thickening agent for savoury dishes.

TOMATILLO Also called the Mexican green tomato, this is a tart-tasting fruit wrapped in a papery husk. It is used either raw or cooked to prepare the most popular Mexican green sauces, such as *salsa verde* and *pipián verde*. Choose firm fruit with a dry, tight-fitting husk, which should be removed before use. Tomatillos can occasionally be found fresh in markets and are also available canned in ethnic shops.

TOMATO (JITOMATE) Ripe fresh tomatoes have been essential to many Mexican dishes since pre-Hispanic times. They are one of the main ingredients of the famous *salsa mexicana* and they are also used raw in salads or cooked in soups, sauces and casseroles. Many varieties grow in Mexico, but the most commonly used are the round tomato (*jitomate bola*) and the plum tomato (*jitomate guaje*).

Essential equipment

Most of the cooking utensils that were used in Mexico before the arrival of the Spanish are still used for preparing traditional Mexican dishes. The grinding stone and grinding pin (*metate* and *mano*), mortar and pestle (*molcajete* and *mano*), the earthenware griddle (*comal*), wooden chocolate whisk (*molinillo*) and wooden tortilla press (*prensa para tortilla*) can still be seen in action in rural areas in the central part of the country. Even though modern kitchens in the cities have substituted the latest culinary gadgets for some of these native tools, the traditional utensils are still kept on view for purely ornamental purposes.

The most sophisticated meals can be made with the simplest equipment, and you can easily make use of everyday pots, pans and tools in your kitchen to prepare each of the recipes in this book. The following equipment is recommended:

BLENDER This is one of the most important cooking utensils in the Mexican kitchen. It is necessary for making smooth chilli mixtures, soups and sauces. It is also used to make sorbets, fruit coolers and Margarita cocktails.

FOOD PROCESSOR This is useful for preparing chunky sauces. It is also important for grinding relatively large quantities of spices and seeds.

MORTAR AND PESTLE This is ideal for grinding small amounts of spices and seeds, and a set should be kept solely for that purpose.

MEDIUM- AND FINE-MESH SIEVES These are indispensable for straining blended chilli mixtures and sauces and separating solids from liquids. A flexible nylon sieve is preferable for using with acidic ingredients, such as raspberries or tomatoes, which may react with the metal and taint or discolour the purée.

HEAVY-BASED SAUCEPAN This is excellent for cooking, as it conducts heat efficiently and evenly.

LARGE HEAVY-BASED FRYING PAN This is indispensable for frying or sautéeing food, for even heat distribution over a high heat, and for roasting chillies, tomatoes, onions and garlic (see page 14), as well as cooking and warming tortillas.

LARGE CAST-IRON STOVE-TOP GRIDDLE PAN This is used for chargrilling meat, fish or vegetables.

KITCHEN KNIVES A large cook's knife with a 20 cm (8 inch) blade is essential for chopping and slicing, while a small cook's knife with a 10 cm (4 inch) blade is ideal for preparing small ingredients and a serrated knife is best for cutting tomatoes and fruit.

METAL KITCHEN TONGS These are a must-have for roasting fresh chillies directly over the high flame of a gas hob.

Techniques

Each recipe in this book provides a description of how to prepare the ingredients. However, a more in-depth explanation is given here to highlight some of the key techniques that are used in Mexican cooking, in order to bring out the authentic flavours and textures of the ingredients.

Preparing dried chillies for sauces

Always remove the stems, then tear the chillies open and remove the seeds, as well as all the light-coloured veins, in order to give a milder flavour. Roast the chillies in a dry heavy-based frying pan over a medium heat for a few seconds on both sides to bring out their flavours. Then soak them in boiling water for 15–20 minutes until soft, stirring frequently to ensure even soaking. Drain the chillies, transfer to a blender or food processor with some of the soaking liquid and blend until smooth. Reserve or discard the remaining liquid, according to the recipe. Pass the chilli mixture through a sieve; this is a very important step, not only to achieve the right texture, but to make the sauces easy to digest. Cook the chilli mixture according to the instructions for each recipe.

Roasting fresh chillies

The purpose of roasting chillies, like fresh *poblanos,* is to remove their skins. Roast the whole chillies directly over a high flame of a gas hob or in a dry heavy-based frying pan. Use metal kitchen tongs to keep turning them until the skins are charred and blistered, place the roasted chillies in a plastic bag, wrap the bag in a tea towel and leave for at least 15 minutes – this helps to loosen their skins. Remove the skins and rinse the chillies under cold running water. Slit the chillies lengthways, discard the stems, seeds and veins and pat dry.

Roasting tomatoes, onions and garlic

Roasting vegetables so that they are slightly charred and partly cooked intensifies their flavours. Heat a dry heavy-based frying pan over a medium heat, lay the unpeeled tomatoes, onion, thickly sliced, and whole garlic cloves on the hot surface and roast them, turning occasionally, until soft.

Preparing spices, seeds and nuts

It is common in Mexico to work with whole spices, almost always toasted and then ground to a dust just before use. Toast the spices in a dry heavy-based frying pan over a medium heat for just a few seconds. This is done not only to intensify their flavour, but to awaken their aroma. In the same way, seeds and nuts can be toasted for a deeper flavour and then left whole, chopped or ground as required.

Menu plan
From the mouth-watering selection of snacks, starters, main meals and desserts presented in this book, you can put together a menu to suit every occasion, from simple family meals to dinner parties, barbecues or Sunday lunches. Whatever the meal, gather your friends and family around the table to share and enjoy this exciting and nutritious food.

LIGHT LUNCH

Baby spinach and mushroom salad (*see page 120*)

Green bean omelette with pasilla chilli sauce (*see page 79*)

Quince paste with manchego cheese (*see page 129*)

FAMILY MEAL

Tlalpan-style broth (*see page 42*)

Meatballs in chipotle sauce (*see page 92*)

Mexican-style rice (*see page 40*)

Sweet potato and pineapple dessert (*see page 132*)

FORMAL LUNCH

Duck tacos (*see page 86*)

Seafood casserole (*see page 64*)

White rice (omit the poblano chilli strips) (*see page 41*)

Raspberry sorbet (*see page 138*)

WEEKEND BREAKFAST

Hot chocolate (*see page 156*)

Black bean open sandwiches (*see page 26*)

'Rabo de mestiza' poached eggs (*see page 78*)

Fresh fruit jelly (*see page 134*)

SUNDAY LUNCH

Fish and nopalitos salad (*see page 32*)

Tortilla soup (*see page 54*)

Pork fillet in pumpkin seed sauce (*see page 96*)

Crème caramel (*see page 126*)

SUMMER LUNCH PARTY

Guacamole with totopos (*see page 28*)

Green rice with langoustines (*see page 38*)

Beef brochettes with salsa mexicana (*see page 90*)

Nopalitos salad (*see page 116*)

Pickled vegetables (*see page 118*)

Corn cake (*see page 136*)

LARGE GATHERING

Guacamole with totopos (*see page 28*)

Pork pozole casserole with red sauce (*see page 95*)

Mango sorbet (*see page 140*)

Walnut jamoncillo (*see page 133*)

DINNER PARTY

Scallop tostadas (*see page 34*)

Black bean soup (*see page 46*)

Halibut fillets with dried chilli sauce (*see page 66*)

White rice (omit the poblano chilli strips) (*see page 41*)

Roasted wild berries (*see page 130*)

Snacks and starters

Lime-marinated prawns

Mexico's love affair with prawns is reflected in the multitude of regional dishes that feature this wonderful shellfish. In this recipe, good-quality prawns are marinated in freshly squeezed lime juice and enlivened with the kick of chillies.

INGREDIENTS *400 g (13 oz) cooked peeled prawns* ‖ *¼ onion, finely chopped* ‖ *3 green chillies, finely chopped (deseeded for a milder taste)* ‖ *3 tablespoons freshly squeezed lime juice* ‖ *3 tablespoons extra virgin olive oil* ‖ *a few drops of Worcestershire sauce (optional)* ‖ *1 tablespoon finely chopped fresh coriander leaves* ‖ *salt and freshly ground black pepper* ‖ *Totopos (see page 28), to serve*

ONE Arrange the prawns on a chilled serving plate. Scatter the onion and chillies on top, then drizzle with the lime juice and oil. Sprinkle over the Worcestershire sauce, if using, and season to taste with salt and pepper. Scatter the coriander on top. **TWO** Serve cold with Totopos (see page 28).

Serves 4

NUTRIENT ANALYSIS PER SERVING 780 kJ – 187 kcal – 23 g protein – 1 g carbohydrate – 1 g sugars – 10 g fat – 2 g saturates – 0 g fibre – 1590 mg sodium

HEALTHY TIP Prawns are naturally low in saturated fat and also contain a number of essential nutrients such as magnesium, selenium and zinc. Limes are an excellent source of vitamin C; they are a potent antiseptic and help to fight colds, coughs and sore throats.

Stuffed jalapeño chillies with tuna

Jalapeño chillies, the dark green chillies from Jalapa, the capital of the east central state of Veracruz, can be hot or very hot and are used all over the country to prepare hot salsas. These famous 'stuffed jalapeños' are traditionally prepared in Mexico City during Lent, and make a great snack any time of the year.

INGREDIENTS *12 large jalapeño chillies* ‖ *750 ml (1¼ pints) water* ‖ *2 tablespoons cider vinegar* ‖ *½ tablespoon salt* ‖ *5 tablespoons soft light brown sugar* ‖ *1 tablespoon olive oil* ‖ *¼ onion, finely chopped* ‖ *1 garlic clove, finely chopped* ‖ *2 tomatoes, skinned, deseeded and chopped* ‖ *200 g (7 oz) can tuna steak in olive oil, well drained and flaked* ‖ *1 bay leaf* ‖ *5 green olives, pitted and chopped* ‖ *1 teaspoon chopped flat leaf parsley leaves* ‖ *salt and freshly ground black pepper*

ONE Wearing rubber gloves (to avoid irritating your skin), use a sharp knife to make a vertical slit down the length of each chilli and carefully remove the seeds and veins. **TWO** Put the measured water in a large saucepan with the vinegar, salt and sugar and bring to the boil. Add the chillies and boil for 5 minutes. Remove the pan from the heat, drain the chillies and transfer to a bowl of fresh cold water. **THREE** Heat the oil in a heavy-based saucepan over a medium heat and sauté the onion until soft. Add the garlic and sauté for a further minute. Add the tomatoes and simmer gently for about 5 minutes, stirring constantly. Add the tuna, bay leaf, olives and parsley, and season to taste with salt and pepper. Simmer for about 10 minutes until the mixture thickens and looks dry. Leave to cool. **FOUR** Drain the chillies well and pat dry. Carefully stuff with the tuna mixture. Arrange the stuffed chillies on a plate and serve at room temperature.

Serves 4

NUTRIENT ANALYSIS PER SERVING 978 kJ – 230 kcal – 18 g protein – 23 g carbohydrate – 22 g sugars – 9 g fat – 1 g saturates – 1 g fibre – 490 mg sodium

HEALTHY TIP Chillies are an excellent source of the powerful antioxidant vitamin C. They also provide minerals including molybdenum, manganese, phosphorous, potassium, thiamine and copper. They stimulate the appetite and digestive system, and are good for the heart and circulation. Tuna is rich in vitamin D and omega-3 fatty acids – excellent for the cardiovascular system.

Mushroom quesadillas

Quesadillas are a typical *antojito* – an informal savoury snack served before the main meal. They consist of corn tortillas filled with a variety of ingredients, such as cheese, sautéed mushrooms, potatoes with chorizo or shredded meat, to mention but a few. Folded over half-moon-style, they can be pan-fried in a little oil or cooked in a dry frying pan, as in this recipe.

INGREDIENTS *2 tablespoons olive oil* ‖ *100 g (3½ oz) onion, finely chopped* ‖ *2 green chillies, finely chopped* ‖ *2 garlic cloves, crushed* ‖ *500 g (1 lb) mushrooms, a mixture of wild and cultivated, roughly chopped* ‖ *1 teaspoon lime juice* ‖ *1 teaspoon finely chopped fresh epazote (if available) or 1 tablespoon finely chopped flat leaf parsley* ‖ *8 soft corn tortillas* ‖ *salt and freshly ground black pepper*

ONE Heat the oil in a heavy-based frying pan over a gentle heat and sauté the onions until soft. **TWO** Add the chillies and garlic and sauté for 1 minute. Add the mushrooms and sauté for a few seconds over a medium-high heat. Add the lime juice and epazote or parsley, season to taste with salt and pepper and cook for a further 5 minutes, or until the mushrooms are just cooked. **THREE** Preheat a large, dry heavy-based frying pan over a medium heat. Warm each side of the tortillas, 2–3 at a time, in the hot pan for about 30 seconds until soft. Place some of the mushroom mixture on one half of each tortilla, then fold over the other half, pressing it down for a few seconds. Turn over and cook until the tortillas become slightly crisp. Transfer to a warm platter and cover with a clean tea towel while you repeat with the remaining tortillas and filling. Serve immediately.

Serves 4

NUTRIENT ANALYSIS PER SERVING 1425 kJ – 339 kcal – 11 g protein – 48 g carbohydrate – 2 g sugars – 12 g fat – 1 g saturates – 6 g fibre – 220 mg sodium

HEALTHY TIP Mushrooms are an excellent source of minerals such as selenium, copper, potassium, phosphorous and zinc. They are also a good source of B-complex vitamins.

Grilled panela cheese with oregano

Panela, a fresh white cheese, is very popular in the states of central Mexico; it can be eaten alone as an *antojito* (snack) or crumbled over a great variety of dishes. Buffalo mozzarella is a good alternative for this recipe.

INGREDIENTS *250 g (8 oz) panela or buffalo mozzarella cheese* ‖ *2 tablespoons extra virgin olive oil* ‖ *1 teaspoon dried oregano* ‖ *salt and freshly ground black pepper* ‖ *warm tortillas, Totopos (see page 28) or sliced crusty bread, to serve*

ONE Slice the panela or mozzarella, arrange the slices in a 15 cm (6 inch) round earthenware or ovenproof dish and season to taste with salt and pepper. Drizzle the oil over the cheese and scatter the oregano on top. **TWO** Bake the cheese in the centre of a preheated oven, 180°C (350°F), Gas Mark 4, for 7–8 minutes. **THREE** Serve hot with warm tortillas, Totopos (see page 28) or sliced crusty bread.

Serves 4

NUTRIENT ANALYSIS PER SERVING 965 kJ – 230 kcal – 16 g protein – 00 g carbohydrate – 0 g sugars – 19 g fat – 9 g saturates – 0 g fibre – 380 mg sodium

HEALTHY TIP Low in fat relative to other cheeses, panela and buffalo mozzarella are an excellent source of calcium, vital in the building of healthy bones and teeth.

Sincronizadas with salsa mexicana

This delicious snack consists of a ham and cheese filling sandwiched between two wheat flour tortillas. These tortillas are mostly used in the northern states of Mexico where maize does not grow very easily. They have probably been made since the end of the 16th century, when wheat was first introduced to Mexico.

INGREDIENTS *2 wheat flour tortillas* ‖ *1 teaspoon vegetable oil* ‖ *125 g (4 oz) mild Cheddar cheese, sliced* ‖ *75 g (3 oz) good-quality ham, sliced* ‖ *Salsa Mexicana (see page 90), to serve*

ONE First, make the Salsa Mexicana (see page 90) and keep at room temperature. **TWO** To make the sincronizadas, brush one side of each tortilla with the oil. Place one tortilla on a work surface with the oiled side down. Arrange half the cheese on top, followed by the ham and the remaining cheese. Place the remaining tortilla on top, with the oiled side uppermost. **THREE** Preheat a large stove-top griddle pan or heavy-based frying pan. Place the sincronizada on the hot surface and cook over a medium heat for about 1½ minutes until the cheese starts to melt. Carefully turn over and cook for a further minute until all the cheese has melted and the tortillas are slightly golden and crispy. **FOUR** Transfer to a plate and cut into 8 triangles. Serve immediately with a side serving of the salsa.

Serves 2

NUTRIENT ANALYSIS PER SERVING 1738 kJ – 416 kcal – 26 g protein – 24 g carbohydrate – 1 g sugars – 25 g fat – 14 g saturates – 1 g fibre – 980 mg sodium

HEALTHY TIP If you want to reduce your fat intake, use buffalo mozzarella cheese instead of Cheddar and replace the ham with cooked turkey, but do not omit the healthy salsa mexicana, made with tomatoes, which is low in calories and rich in vitamin C and other nutrients.

Black bean open sandwiches

Beans are a very important source of protein in the Mexican diet. They are prepared in many different ways and served at any time of the day. *Molletes* such as these – open crusty bread rolls filled with refried beans topped with melted cheese – are often served for breakfast or a light dinner in Mexico City cafeterias, usually accompanied by salsa mexicana.

INGREDIENTS *4 crusty bread rolls or 8 slices French bread ‖ 20 g (¾ oz) unsalted butter ‖ 50 g (2 oz) mild Cheddar cheese, grated ‖ Salsa Mexicana (see page 90), to serve ‖ finely chopped red chilli, to garnish (optional) ‖ finely chopped fresh coriander, to garnish (optional)*

REFRIED BEANS *250 g (8 oz) dried black beans ‖ 1.5 litres (2½ pints) cold water ‖ 1 small onion, halved ‖ 2 garlic cloves, peeled ‖ 1 fresh epazote sprig (if available) ‖ ½ teaspoon salt ‖ 2 tablespoons vegetable oil*

ONE First make the refried beans. Put the beans in a large saucepan, add cold water to cover by 12–15 cm (5–6 inches) and leave to soak overnight (8–12 hours). **TWO** Drain the beans, rinse and cover with the measured cold water. Add the onion, garlic cloves and epazote sprig. Bring to the boil, then reduce the heat and simmer, partially covered, for 2–3 hours until the beans are soft. Check frequently: if the beans appear above the water level during the cooking time, add boiling water (never use cold water) to cover. **THREE** Remove the onion, garlic and epazote and add the salt. Drain the beans and purée in a blender or food processor, or mash with a potato masher while still warm. Heat the oil in a heavy-based saucepan over a medium heat, add the beans and cook until dry, stirring constantly. Remove from the heat and leave to cool – the bean purée will thicken. **FOUR** Cut the bread rolls in half horizontally and remove some of the soft inside crumb. Spread with the butter, add the refried beans on top and sprinkle with the cheese. Place on a baking sheet and bake in a preheated oven, 180°C (350°F), Gas Mark 4, for 6–8 minutes until the cheese has melted and the bread is lightly toasted. **FIVE** Scatter over the chilli and coriander, if liked, then serve hot with Salsa Mexicana (see page 90).

Serves 4

NUTRIENT ANALYSIS PER SERVING 1890 kJ – 448 kcal – 23 g protein – 57 g carbohydrate – 3 g sugars – 16 g fat – 6 g saturates – 17 g fibre – 660 mg sodium

HEALTHY TIP Well known for their high nutritional value, black beans are a very good source of protein, carbohydrates, calcium, iron, manganese and phosphorus, as well as many other minerals and vitamins. They are also an excellent source of dietary fibre and amino acids.

Guacamole with totopos

Crisp and lightly salted *totopos* are fried corn tortilla triangles usually served to accompany refried beans or guacamole, the ever-popular avocado salsa flavoured with green chillies, onions and fresh coriander. This Mexican speciality is prepared all over the country and can be served as a side dish to grilled meats, salads and rice or simply spooned over any kind of taco.

INGREDIENTS *2 large ripe avocados* ‖ *1 tablespoon finely chopped onion* ‖ *2 serrano or jalapeño chillies, finely chopped* ‖ *2 tablespoons finely chopped fresh coriander leaves, plus extra leaves to garnish* ‖ *a few drops of freshly squeezed lime juice* ‖ *salt*
TOTOPOS *6 soft corn tortillas* ‖ *vegetable oil, for brushing* ‖ *salt*

ONE To make the totopos, brush each side of the tortillas with a little oil and cut into triangles. Arrange on a baking sheet and bake in a preheated oven, 180°C (350°F), Gas Mark 4, for 8–10 minutes until crisp. Sprinkle with a little salt and leave to cool on a wire rack. **TWO** Halve the avocados and remove the stones. Cut the flesh into 1 cm (½ inch) cubes, then use a spoon to scoop out the remaining flesh from the skin and put in a bowl. **THREE** Add the onion, chillies and coriander to the bowl and mix together gently, making sure that you don't squash the avocado. Add the lime juice and season to taste with salt. Garnish with coriander leaves and serve immediately with the totopos.

Serves 4

NUTRIENT ANALYSIS PER SERVING 1607 kJ – 385 kcal – 8 g protein – 37 g carbohydrate – 1 g sugars – 23 g fat – 4 g saturates – 2 g fibre – 167 mg sodium
HEALTHY TIP Avocados contain a wide variety of nutrients including vitamins and minerals, as well as heart-healthy monounsaturated fat. High in vitamin E, they are easily digested and help to prevent anaemia. Fresh coriander has antibiotic properties and helps to relieve digestive problems.

Tiger prawn taquitos

Tacos, a favourite Mexican *antojito* (snack), are filled and rolled-up soft corn tortillas. There are no limits to the type of fillings and they vary according to the region, but they are usually served with a hot chilli sauce. These mouthwatering prawn *taquitos* are traditionally served in Baja California and the states of the northern Pacific Coast.

INGREDIENTS *2 tablespoons olive oil* ‖ *1 onion, thinly sliced lengthways* ‖ *500 g (1 lb) uncooked tiger prawns, peeled and deveined* ‖ *2 garlic cloves, crushed* ‖ *4 serrano chillies, deseeded and sliced into thin strips* ‖ *1 tablespoon chopped fresh coriander* ‖ *8 soft corn tortillas* ‖ *salt and freshly ground black pepper* ‖ *Guacamole (see page 28) or your favourite salsa, to serve* ‖ *fresh coriander, to garnish*

ONE Heat the oil in a frying pan over a gentle heat and sauté the onion for 1 minute. **TWO** Add the prawns, garlic and chillies and sauté for about 3 minutes – the prawns are cooked when they turn pink and curl up. Season to taste with salt and pepper and scatter the coriander on top. Keep warm. **THREE** Preheat a large, dry heavy-based frying pan over a medium heat. Warm each side of the tortillas, 2–3 at a time, in the hot pan for about 30 seconds until soft. Place some of the prawn mixture in the centre of each tortilla and roll up. Transfer to a warm platter and cover with a clean tea towel while you repeat with the remaining tortillas and prawn mixture. **FOUR** Serve immediately with Guacamole (see page 28) or your favourite salsa, garnished with fresh coriander.

Serves 4

NUTRIENT ANALYSIS PER SERVING 1750 kJ – 416 kcal – 30 g protein – 47 g carbohydrate – 1 g sugars – 12 g fat – 1 g saturates – 3 g fibre – 480 mg sodium

HEALTHY TIP Prawns are a good source of protein, highly nutritious and easy to digest. Chillies contain vitamin C and capsaicin, and are recommended for circulatory and digestive problems.

Fish and nopalitos salad

This is a typical Mexican starter made with marinated fish and inspired by the traditional recipe of ceviche from Zihuatanejo in the state of Guerrero on the Pacific Coast. The nopales, the fleshy oval leaves of the nopal cactus, add a delicate texture and slightly tart flavour.

INGREDIENTS *350 g (11 ½ oz) cod or sole fillets, skinned, rinsed and patted dry ‖ 2 red chillies, deseeded and finely sliced ‖ 2 green chillies, deseeded and finely sliced ‖ 1 red onion, finely sliced lengthways ‖ 100 ml (3 ½ fl oz) freshly squeezed lime juice ‖ 200 g (7 oz) cooked fresh nopales, cut into strips ‖ 4 radishes, finely sliced ‖ salt and freshly ground black pepper ‖ fresh coriander leaves, to garnish ‖ Totopos (see page 28), to serve*

DRESSING *60 ml (2 ½ fl oz) extra virgin olive oil ‖ 20 ml (¾ fl oz) freshly squeezed lime juice, or to taste ‖ ½ teaspoon clear honey ‖ ½ teaspoon dried oregano ‖ salt*

ONE Cut the fish into 1 x 4 cm (½ x 1½ inch) strips. Put in a glass bowl with the chillies and onion. Add the lime juice and season with salt and pepper. Cover and leave to marinate in the refrigerator for 1 hour. **TWO** Drain the excess lime juice and add the nopales and radishes. Mix all the dressing ingredients together well and pour over the fish mixture. Check the seasoning. **THREE** To serve, divide the fish and nopalitos salad between 4 plates. Garnish with coriander leaves and add a couple of Totopos (see page 28) on the side of each serving.

Serves 4

NUTRIENT ANALYSIS PER SERVING 825 kJ – 198 kcal – 17 g protein – 6 g carbohydrate – 4 g sugars – 12 g fat – 2 g saturates – 2 g fibre – 80 mg sodium

HEALTHY TIP An excellent source of vitamin A and C, nopales are also a good source of the B vitamins and calcium. Cod is a good source of vitamins B6 and 12, and is also beneficial for cardiovascular health. (If possible, try to use cod from sustainable sources or farmed cod.) Sole is a good source of selenium, potassium and vitamins B6 and B12.

Scallop tostadas

A delicate and tasty starter made with fresh scallops placed on a tostada, a crunchy corn tortilla. A tostada is a typical *antojito* (snack), popular throughout Mexico. It can be either eaten plain or topped with fresh ingredients that vary according to the region.

INGREDIENTS *200 g (7 oz) uncooked scallops, white flesh only* ‖ *30 g (1 oz) red onion, finely sliced* ‖ *2 jalapeño chillies, deseeded and finely sliced* ‖ *10 cm (4 inch) piece of cucumber, deseeded and cut into cubes* ‖ *2 teaspoons finely chopped chives* ‖ *2 tablespoons freshly squeezed lime juice* ‖ *2 tablespoons extra virgin olive oil* ‖ *4 soft corn tortillas, preferably small* ‖ *salt and freshly ground black pepper*
TO GARNISH *fresh coriander leaves* ‖ *lime wedges*

ONE Slice each scallop into 3–4 equal pieces about 5 mm (¼ inch) thick and place in a glass bowl. Add the red onion, chillies, cucumber and chives. Gently stir and mix with the lime juice and oil. Season to taste with salt and pepper. Cover and leave to marinate in the refrigerator for 20 minutes. **TWO** If you cannot find small corn tortillas, use a 10–12 cm (4–5 inch) round pastry cutter to cut out rounds from large corn tortillas. Place the tortillas on a baking sheet and bake in a preheated oven, 180°C (350°F), Gas Mark 4, for 8–10 minutes until crisp. Leave to cool before using. **THREE** Assemble the tostadas just before serving. Using a slotted spoon, place a quarter of the scallop mixture on top of each tostada. Garnish with coriander leaves and lime wedges and serve immediately.

Serves 4

NUTRIENT ANALYSIS PER SERVING (using small tortillas or cut small rounds, weighing approximately 17 g (½ oz) each) 727 kJ – 173 kcal – 14 g protein – 13 g carbohydrate – 1 g sugars – 8 g fat – 1 g saturates – 1 g fibre – 139 mg sodium

HEALTHY TIP Crisping the tortillas in the oven rather than deep-frying them, as is traditionally the cooking method, makes these tostadas even healthier.

Soups and rice

Green rice with langoustines

The combination of rice and shellfish is much loved in Mexico. Here, fragrant basmati rice is coloured green with coriander and spinach, seasoned with a poblano chilli and served with langoustines to offer a delicious combination of flavours and textures.

INGREDIENTS *325 g (11 oz) basmati rice* ‖ *1 poblano chilli* ‖ *25 g (1 oz) fresh coriander* ‖ *25 g (1 oz) spinach* ‖ *¼ onion* ‖ *1 garlic clove* ‖ *500 ml (17 fl oz) chicken stock* ‖ *2 tablespoons vegetable oil* ‖ *3 garlic cloves, crushed* ‖ *1 tablespoon olive oil* ‖ *8 uncooked langoustines, in their shells, legs removed, or 8 uncooked jumbo tiger prawns, in their shells, deveined and legs removed* ‖ *salt and freshly ground black pepper*

ONE Soak the rice in hot water for 15 minutes. Drain, rinse well and drain again. **TWO** Carefully hold the chilli over a high gas flame with metal kitchen tongs or put in a preheated dry heavy-based frying pan over a high heat, turning frequently, until the skin is charred. Put the roasted chilli in a plastic bag, wrap the bag with a tea towel and leave to sweat for at least 15 minutes. Remove the skin, discard the stem and seeds, rinse and pat dry. **THREE** Put the chilli, coriander, spinach, onion and whole garlic in a blender or food processor and blend until a fairly smooth texture. **FOUR** Cook the mixture in a heavy-based saucepan over a medium heat for about 8 minutes, stirring constantly. Add the stock, bring to the boil and season to taste with salt. Keep warm. **FIVE** Heat the vegetable oil in a heavy-based saucepan over a medium heat and sauté the rice, stirring constantly, for about 5 minutes, or until it loses its stickiness. Add the chilli and stock mixture and bring to the boil, stirring. Reduce the heat to low, cover and cook for about 10 minutes, or until the liquid has been absorbed and the rice is tender. Remove from the heat and leave to rest for 10 minutes. **SIX** Mix the crushed garlic, olive oil and a little salt together to make a paste. Heat a wok or a heavy-based frying pan over a high heat and sauté the langoustines or jumbo tiger prawns with the garlic paste for a few minutes. Turn the langoustines or prawns over and cook on the other side for a further minute until cooked through. **SEVEN** Transfer the rice to a warm platter and arrange the langoustines on top. Season to taste with pepper and serve immediately.

Serves 4

NUTRIENT ANALYSIS PER SERVING 1643 kJ – 394 kcal – 11 g protein – 67 g carbohydrate – 1 g sugars – 9 g fat – 1 g saturates – 2 g fibre – 253 mg sodium

HEALTHY TIP Langoustines are highly nutritious and easy to digest. They are an excellent source of protein as well as selenium, an antioxidant that protects from heart disease and is vital for a healthy immune system.

Mexican-style rice

Rice plays an important part in the Mexican diet. It is traditionally served at lunchtime between the soup and the main dish, especially in Mexico City. It is also served as a garnish to many dishes. Mexican-style – *a la mexicana* – is one of the popular ways to prepare rice; it is first fried, then seasoned with tomato and cooked with carrots, peas and whole green chillies.

INGREDIENTS *325 g (11 oz) basmati rice ‖ 200 g (7 oz) tomatoes ‖ ¼ onion ‖ 1 garlic clove, peeled ‖ 2½ tablespoons vegetable oil ‖ 500 ml (17 fl oz) chicken stock ‖ 50 g (2 oz) carrot, diced ‖ 50 g (2 oz) shelled fresh or frozen peas ‖ 4 green chillies ‖ 2 flat leaf parsley sprigs ‖ salt*

ONE Soak the rice in hot water for 15 minutes. Drain, rinse well and drain again. **TWO** Put the tomatoes, onion and garlic clove in a blender or food processor and blend to a fairly smooth texture. Pass the mixture through a sieve. **THREE** Heat ½ tablespoon of the oil in a heavy-based saucepan over a medium heat, pour in the tomato mixture and bring to the boil, then reduce the heat and simmer for 8–10 minutes until cooked, stirring constantly. Add the stock, bring to the boil and season to taste with salt. Reduce the heat and keep warm. **FOUR** Heat the remaining oil in a heavy-based saucepan over a medium heat and sauté the rice, stirring constantly, for about 5 minutes, or until it loses its stickiness. Pour in the tomato and stock mixture, add the carrot, peas and chillies and place the parsley sprigs on top. Bring to boil, then reduce the heat, cover and cook over a very low heat for about 10 minutes, or until the liquid has been absorbed and the rice is cooked. Remove from the heat and leave to rest for 10 minutes before serving.

Serves 4

NUTRIENT ANALYSIS PER SERVING 1616 kJ – 387 kcal – 8 g protein – 70 g carbohydrate – 3 g sugars – 8 g fat – 1 g saturates – 4 g fibre – 214 mg sodium

HEALTHY TIP Rice is suitable for people on a gluten-free diet. The vegetables used in this recipe enhance the nutritional value of this energy-providing dish.

White rice with poblano chilli strips

This traditional rice dish is served with the mouth-wateringly delicious chilli poblano strips called *rajas*. They are sautéed with onions and finished with a touch of cream. It is common to serve this rice shaped in a mould to form a large ring, with the *rajas* in the centre.

INGREDIENTS *325 g (11 oz) basmati rice* ‖ *2 tablespoons vegetable oil* ‖ *500 ml (17 fl oz) chicken stock* ‖ *freshly squeezed juice of ½ lime* ‖ *2 flat leaf parsley sprigs* ‖ *salt*
POBLANO CHILLI STRIPS *3 poblano chillies* ‖ *1 onion, sliced lengthways* ‖ *1 tablespoon vegetable oil* ‖ *60 ml (2½ fl oz) double cream* ‖ *salt*

ONE Soak the rice in hot water for 15 minutes. Drain, rinse well and drain again. **TWO** Heat the oil in a heavy-based saucepan over a medium heat and sauté the rice, stirring constantly, for about 5 minutes, or until it loses its stickiness. Add the stock, bring to the boil, season with salt and add the lime juice and parsley sprigs. Cover and cook over a low heat for about 10 minutes, or until the liquid has been absorbed and the rice is cooked. Remove from the heat and leave to rest for 10 minutes. **THREE** To make the poblano chilli strips, carefully hold the chillies over a high gas flame with metal kitchen tongs or put in a preheated dry heavy-based frying pan over a high heat, turning frequently, until the skins are charred. Put the roasted chillies in a plastic bag, wrap the bag with a tea towel and leave for at least 15 minutes. Remove the skins, rinse the chillies under cold running water and discard the stems and seeds. Pat dry and slice lengthways into strips. **FOUR** Heat the oil in a heavy-based saucepan over a medium heat and sauté the onion until soft. Add the chilli strips and sauté for 10 minutes, stirring occasionally. Season to taste with salt. Just before serving, stir in the cream, then check the seasoning. **FIVE** To serve, transfer the rice to a warm platter and top with the chilli strips.

Serves 4

NUTRIENT ANALYSIS PER SERVING 1870 kJ – 450 kcal – 7 g protein – 68 g carbohydrate – 3 g sugars – 16 g fat – 5 g saturates – 2 g fibre – 213 mg sodium
HEALTHY TIP Onions have long been recognized for their medicinal value. They are a very good source of vitamin C and dietary fibre. Both onions and chillies reduce blood cholesterol and the risk of blood clots. They are also very important for the immune system. To reduce the fat content of this dish further, serve the poblano chilli strips without the cream.

Tlalpan-style broth

Soups are an integral part of the Mexican diet. In central Mexico, lunch generally starts with a soup followed by rice and a main course with vegetables. This broth contains a healthy combination of chicken, chickpeas, carrots and avocado, which marries beautifully with the smoky chipotle chilli.

INGREDIENTS *1.5 litres (2½ pints) chicken stock* ‖ *175 g (6 oz) boneless, skinless chicken breast* ‖ *1 tablespoon vegetable oil* ‖ *1 onion, finely chopped* ‖ *2 carrots, peeled and diced* ‖ *2 garlic cloves, finely chopped* ‖ *400 g (13 oz) cooked chickpeas* ‖ *1 chipotle chilli, bottled or canned in adobo sauce, deseeded and cut into strips* ‖ *1 large ripe avocado, stoned, peeled and diced* ‖ *2 tablespoons chopped fresh coriander* ‖ *salt* ‖ *1 lime, cut into wedges, to serve*

ONE Put the stock and chicken in a saucepan and bring to the boil. Reduce the heat to medium and simmer for about 20 minutes until the chicken is cooked. Remove the chicken from the stock, reserving the stock, and leave to cool. Shred the chicken and set aside. **TWO** Heat the oil in a large saucepan over a medium heat and sauté the onion and carrots until the onion is translucent. Add the garlic and cook for a further minute. Pour in the reserved stock and simmer for 10 minutes. Add the chickpeas and simmer for a further 10 minutes. Season to taste with salt. **THREE** Just before serving, add the chilli and shredded chicken to the broth and heat through. Pour the broth into warm bowls and sprinkle over the avocado and coriander. Serve with the lime wedges on the side.

Serves 4

NUTRIENT ANALYSIS PER SERVING 1354 kJ – 324 kcal – 20 g protein – 25 g carbohydrate – 6 g sugars – 16 g fat – 3 g saturates – 7 g fibre – 257 mg sodium

HEALTHY TIP This is a highly nutritious chicken and vegetable soup. To mention just a few of the health benefits, chickpeas are an excellent source of complex carbohydrates and dietary fibre. They also provide protein, vitamins and minerals such as calcium, potassium and iron, as well as having antiseptic and diuretic properties.

Poblano chilli soup with prawns

The elegant poblano chilli, with its thick flesh and delicious flavour, is perhaps one of the most widely used chillies in Mexico, mainly in the states in the centre of the country. This versatile chilli features in countless dishes and sauces.

INGREDIENTS *6 poblano chillies* ‖ *1 tablespoon vegetable oil* ‖ *½ onion, roughly chopped* ‖ *1.5 litres (2½ pints) chicken stock* ‖ *150 g (5 oz) cooked peeled prawns* ‖ *salt and freshly ground black pepper*

ONE Carefully hold the chillies over a high gas flame with metal kitchen tongs or put in a preheated dry heavy-based frying pan over a high heat, turning frequently, until the skins are charred. Put the roasted chillies in a plastic bag, wrap the bag with a tea towel and leave to sweat for at least 15 minutes. Remove the skins, rinse the chillies under cold running water and discard the stems and seeds. Pat dry and slice lengthways into strips. **TWO** Heat the oil in a large heavy-based saucepan over a medium heat and sauté the onion until soft. Add the chillies and sauté for a few minutes, stirring constantly. Add some of the stock and bring to the boil, then reduce the heat and simmer for about 5 minutes. **THREE** Purée the chilli mixture in a blender or food processor until smooth and return to the saucepan. Add the remaining stock and simmer for 10–15 minutes. Season to taste with salt and pepper. **FOUR** Reserve 4–6 whole prawns for garnish, chop the remaining prawns and add to the soup just before serving. Serve hot, garnished with the reserved whole prawns.

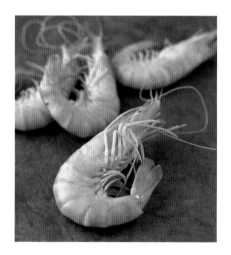

Serves 4

NUTRIENT ANALYSIS PER SERVING 360 kJ – 86 kcal – 10 g protein – 3 g carbohydrate – 3 g sugars – 4 g fat – 0 g saturates – 0 g fibre – 800 mg sodium

HEALTHY TIP Chillies are an excellent source of capsaicin, an antioxidant, pain reliever and anti-inflammatory agent. Capsaicin may also reduce blood cholesterol and the risk of blood clots. It stimulates the appetite and the digestive system.

Walnut soup with chipotle chilli

This elegant soup with its delicious and delicate flavour is served on special occasions. The combination of walnuts and chipotle chillies gives the soup a distinctive flavour, making it a great favourite.

INGREDIENTS *2 chipotle chillies* ‖ *1 tablespoon vegetable oil* ‖ *½ onion, chopped* ‖ *1–2 garlic cloves, chopped* ‖ *2 tomatoes, chopped* ‖ *1.5 litres (2½ pints) chicken stock* ‖ *200 g (7 oz) walnuts, ground, plus extra, roughly chopped, to garnish* ‖ *salt and freshly ground black pepper* ‖ *flat leaf parsley, to garnish (optional)*

ONE Remove the stem from the chillies and discard the seeds (for a milder sauce, remove all the stringy, light-coloured veins as well). Put in a dry heavy-based frying pan over a medium heat and lightly roast for a few seconds on both sides. Soak in boiling water for 15–20 minutes until soft. **TWO** Heat the oil in a large saucepan over a medium heat and sauté the onion until soft. Add the garlic and sauté for a further minute. Add the tomatoes and cook for a few minutes, stirring constantly. **THREE** Drain the chillies and transfer to a blender or food processor with the tomato mixture. Add 250 ml (8 fl oz) of the stock and blend to a fairly smooth texture, then pass through a sieve. **FOUR** Return the tomato and chilli mixture to the saucepan and simmer gently for 10–15 minutes until cooked. Season to taste with salt and pepper. **FIVE** Blend the ground walnuts with some of the remaining stock until smooth. Add to the tomato mixture with the remaining stock and bring to the boil. Reduce the heat and simmer for 10–15 minutes. Check the seasoning. **SIX** Serve the soup in individual bowls, garnished with chopped walnuts and parsley, if liked.

Serves 4

NUTRIENT ANALYSIS PER SERVING 1780 kJ – 430 kcal – 9 g protein – 5 g carbohydrate – 4 g sugars – 42 g fat – 4 g saturates – 4 g fibre – 214 mg sodium

HEALTHY TIP Walnuts have cholesterol-lowering properties and are an excellent source of omega-3 essential fatty acids. They are also a good source of vitamins A, B and C and minerals such as calcium, copper, iron and manganese. They are excellent for strengthening the immune system.

Black bean soup

Beans are a staple ingredient of Mexican cuisine and are served as starters, soups, salads or as a main dish. Black bean soup is a great favourite, especially when topped with fried tortilla strips and garnished with crumbled white cheese. Here, a hint of dried oregano has been added to enhance the delicious flavour.

INGREDIENTS *250 g (8 oz) dried black beans* ‖ *1.5 litres (2½ pints) cold water* ‖ *1 small onion, halved, and ½ onion, chopped* ‖ *4 garlic cloves, peeled* ‖ *1 fresh epazote sprig (if available)* ‖ *1 teaspoon salt* ‖ *500 ml (17 fl oz) vegetable or chicken stock* ‖ *2 tomatoes, skinned and deseeded* ‖ *1 tablespoon olive oil* ‖ *vegetable oil, for brushing* ‖ *2 soft corn tortillas* ‖ *100 g (3½ oz) feta cheese, diced* ‖ *1 red chilli, deseeded and finely sliced* ‖ *dried oregano, for sprinkling*

ONE Soak the beans in plenty of cold water for 8–12 hours. **TWO** Drain the beans, rinse and cover with the measured cold water. Add the halved onion, 2 of the garlic cloves and the epazote sprig. Bring to the boil, then reduce the heat and simmer, partially covered, for 2–3 hours until the beans are soft. If the beans appear above the water level during the cooking time, add boiling water (never cold water) to cover. **THREE** Remove the onion, garlic and epazote and add the salt. Purée the beans with their cooking water and half of the stock in a blender or food processor, then sieve. Add more stock if the mixture is too thick. **FOUR** Purée the tomatoes with the remaining garlic cloves and the chopped onion in the blender or food processor. Heat the olive oil in a heavy-based saucepan, add the tomato mixture and simmer for 5–8 minutes, stirring constantly. Add the bean mixture and simmer for 10 minutes. Check the seasoning. **FIVE** Brush each side of the tortillas with a little vegetable oil, then cut into thin strips. Spread out on a baking sheet and bake in a preheated oven, 180°C (350°F), Gas Mark 4, for 6–8 minutes until golden. **SIX** Serve the soup in individual bowls, topped with a few tortilla strips. Scatter over the feta and chilli, and sprinkle the oregano on the top.

Serves 4

NUTRIENT ANALYSIS PER SERVING 1463 kJ – 347 kcal – 21 g protein – 45 g carbohydrate – 6 g sugars – 11 g fat – 4 g saturates – 16 g fibre – 1126 mg sodium

HEALTHY TIP Black beans are a very good source of cholesterol-lowering fibre. They also prevent blood sugar levels from rising too rapidly after a meal, great for individuals with diabetes or hypoglycaemia.

Milpa soup

Milpa is the term for a corn field where a great variety of vegetables and fruit are also cultivated. This soup is one of the pre-Hispanic dishes that use vegetables harvested in the *milpa*, such as sweetcorn, courgettes, poblano chillies and green beans, and is flavoured with the herb epazote.

INGREDIENTS *2 poblano chillies* ‖ *1 tablespoon vegetable oil* ‖ *½ onion, finely chopped* ‖ *1 garlic clove, finely chopped* ‖ *250 g (8 oz) fresh sweetcorn kernels* ‖ *2 courgettes, cut into small strips* ‖ *100 g (3½ oz) green beans, cut into pieces* ‖ *1 litre (1¾ pints) chicken stock* ‖ *2 large fresh epazote sprigs (if available) or fresh coriander sprigs* ‖ *salt and freshly ground black pepper*

ONE Carefully hold the chillies over a high gas flame with metal kitchen tongs or put in a preheated dry heavy-based frying pan over a high heat, turning frequently, until the skins are charred. Put the roasted chillies in a plastic bag, wrap the bag with a tea towel and leave to sweat for at least 15 minutes. Remove the skins, rinse the chillies under cold running water and discard the stems and seeds. Pat dry and slice lengthways into strips. **TWO** Heat the oil in a large saucepan over a medium heat and sauté the onion until soft. Add the chillies, garlic and the remaining vegetables and sauté for about 3 minutes, stirring constantly. **THREE** Add the stock and bring to the boil. Add the epazote or coriander sprigs, reduce the heat and simmer gently for about 10 minutes until the vegetables are cooked. Season to taste with salt and pepper. **FOUR** Discard the epazote, if using, and serve the soup hot in bowls.

Serves 4

NUTRIENT ANALYSIS PER SERVING 458 kJ – 109 kcal – 4 g protein – 14 g carbohydrate – 4 g sugars – 5 g fat – 1 g saturates – 3 g fibre – 208 mg sodium

HEALTHY TIP This delicious and nutritious vegetable soup is packed with vitamins, minerals and other nutrients that help to strengthen the immune system. In addition, the vegetables are a good source of dietary fibre.

Chilled avocado soup

Avocados were consumed by the inhabitants of southern Mexico and Central America before the arrival of the Spanish. They were easily accepted in Europe mainly because of their reputation as an aphrodisiac. This delicious and refreshing soup is ideal for a hot summer's day.

INGREDIENTS *2 large ripe avocados, stoned and peeled* | *1 teaspoon freshly squeezed lime juice* | *1 litre (1¾ pints) fresh chicken stock, chilled and solidified fat removed* | *1 teaspoon chopped fresh coriander, plus extra to garnish* | *salt and freshly ground black pepper*

ONE Put the avocados, lime juice, about half the stock and the coriander in a blender or food processor and blend until smooth. **TWO** Pour the avocado mixture into a glass bowl. Add the remaining stock, mix thoroughly and season to taste with salt and pepper. Cover and chill in the refrigerator. **THREE** Serve in individual soup bowls, sprinkled with chopped coriander to garnish.

Serves 4

NUTRIENT ANALYSIS PER SERVING 778 kJ – 189 kcal – 2 g protein – 2 g carbohydrate – 1 g sugars – 19 g fat – 4 g saturates – 0 g fibre – 210 mg sodium

HEALTHY TIP Most of the fats in avocados are health-promoting monounsaturated fats, especially oleic acid. Avocados are rich in vitamin E, which protects cells against the harmful effects of toxins. They also contain a fair amount of vitamin C, thiamine, riboflavin and potassium, the latter a mineral that helps to regulate blood pressure.

Carrot and beetroot soup

A glorious soup made from two humble root vegetables. The colour is in itself a feast for the eyes.

INGREDIENTS *1 tablespoon olive oil* ‖ *400 g (13 oz) carrots, roughly chopped* ‖ *150 g (5 oz) onion, roughly chopped* ‖ *1 leek, white part only, roughly chopped* ‖ *1 garlic clove, crushed* ‖ *1.2 litres (2 pints) vegetable or chicken stock* ‖ *100 g (3½ oz) beetroot, cooked and roughly chopped* ‖ *75 g (3 oz) feta cheese, crumbled* ‖ *2 tablespoons finely chopped fresh coriander* ‖ *salt and freshly ground black pepper* ‖ *griddled corn tortillas, to serve (optional)*

ONE Heat the oil in a large heavy-based saucepan over a gentle heat. Add the carrots, onion and leek, cover and gently sweat for 10 minutes, stirring occasionally. **TWO** Add the garlic and stock and bring to the boil, then reduce the heat and simmer for 20–25 minutes until the carrots are just tender. Leave to cool. **THREE** Transfer to a blender or food processor, add the beetroot and blend until smooth. Return to the saucepan, reheat and season to taste with salt and pepper. **FOUR** Serve in individual bowls, sprinkled with the feta and coriander, with corn tortillas to accompany, if liked.

Serves 4–6

NUTRIENT ANALYSIS PER SERVING 579 kJ – 139 kcal – 5 g protein – 14 g carbohydrate – 12 g sugars – 7 g fat – 3 g saturates – 5 g fibre – 518 mg sodium

HEALTHY TIP Carrots and beetroot are packed with healthy nutrients and are an excellent source of vitamin A and potassium. These two super vegetables are well known for their medicinal properties and for the support they give to the immune system.

Tortilla soup

Also known as 'Aztec soup', this is one of the most delicious and typical soups of central Mexico. The broth is seasoned with the aromatic herb epazote, native to Mesoamerica, which gives a distinctive flavour to the soup. It is typically garnished with cheese, avocado and pasilla chilli rings.

INGREDIENTS *2 medium-large ripe tomatoes, skinned and deseeded ‖ 1 garlic clove, roughly chopped ‖ ½ onion, roughly chopped ‖ 1 tablespoon vegetable oil, plus extra for brushing and frying ‖ 1.5 litres (2½ pints) chicken stock ‖ 3 large fresh epazote sprigs (if available) or fresh coriander sprigs ‖ 8 soft corn tortillas ‖ 2 pasilla chillies ‖ 100 g (3½ oz) feta cheese, diced ‖ 1 large ripe avocado, stoned, peeled and diced ‖ salt and freshly ground black pepper*

ONE Purée the tomatoes in a blender or food processor with the garlic and onion, adding a small amount of the stock if too thick. **TWO** Heat the oil in a large saucepan over a medium heat, add the tomato mixture and cook for 2 minutes. Reduce the heat and simmer gently for about 8 minutes until cooked, stirring constantly. **THREE** Add the stock and bring to the boil. Add the epazote or coriander sprigs, reduce the heat and simmer for about 15 minutes. Discard the epazote or coriander sprigs and season to taste with salt and pepper. **FOUR** Brush both sides of each tortilla with a little oil and cut into thin strips. Spread out on a baking sheet and bake in a preheated oven, 180°C (350°F), Gas Mark 4, for 8–10 minutes until golden brown. **FIVE** Meanwhile, cut the chillies into 5 mm (¼ inch) rings, discarding the seeds. Heat a little oil in a small frying pan and fry the chilli rings for about 10 seconds, or until crisp. Drain on kitchen paper. **SIX** To serve, place an equal quantity of the tortilla strips in the centre of each soup plate, scatter over the feta, avocado and a few chilli rings, then pour over the very hot soup.

Serves 4

NUTRIENT ANALYSIS PER SERVING 2019 kJ – 483 kcal – 13 g protein – 50 g carbohydrate – 3 g sugars – 26 g fat – 6 g saturates – 3 g fibre – 786 mg sodium

HEALTHY TIP This nutritious soup is suitable for people with gluten intolerance, if the tortillas are pure corn (some bought soft corn tortillas may contain wheat gluten), and contains health-promoting tomatoes and avocados, which are rich in vitamins and minerals, and good sources of dietary fibre. They can also help guard against certain cancers and sustain energy levels.

Fish and seafood

Tuna steaks with salsa arriera

There is nothing like a delicious salsa to enhance the magnificent flavour of a seared tuna steak. Traditionally, *salsa arriera* is extremely hot, prepared with chopped onions and chillies marinated in lime juice with a hint of oregano, but there is always the option of making it milder by using fewer chillies and removing their seeds.

INGREDIENTS *4 x 175 g (6 oz) fresh tuna steaks ‖ 1 tablespoon olive oil ‖ 1 garlic clove, crushed ‖ salt and freshly ground black pepper ‖ lime wedges, to garnish or snipped chives, to garnish*

SALSA ARRIERA *100 g (3½ oz) onion, finely chopped ‖ 100 ml (3½ fl oz) freshly squeezed lime juice ‖ 4–5 green chillies, finely chopped (deseeded for a milder taste) ‖ 1 teaspoon dried oregano, or to taste ‖ salt and freshly ground black pepper*

ONE Brush the tuna steaks with the oil and garlic and season with salt and pepper. Cover and chill in the refrigerator for at least 20 minutes. **TWO** Meanwhile, mix all the salsa ingredients together in a glass bowl and leave to stand at room temperature for at least 15 minutes. Check the seasoning. **THREE** Preheat a ridged stove-top griddle pan over a medium-high heat. Add the tuna steaks to the hot pan and cook for 2–3 minutes on each side until cooked – they should be opaque, lightly browned and firm, but still moist. **FOUR** Transfer the tuna steaks to a warm dish and spoon the salsa on top. Serve immediately with lime wedges or garnish with snipped chives.

Serves 4

NUTRIENT ANALYSIS PER SERVING 1185 kJ – 280 kcal – 43 g protein – 3 g carbohydrate – 2 g sugars – 11 g fat – 3 g saturates – 0 g fibre – 85 mg sodium

HEALTHY TIP An excellent source of high-quality protein, tuna is rich in a variety of important nutrients, including the minerals selenium, magnesium and potassium; the B vitamins niacin, B1 and B6; and perhaps, most importantly, the beneficial omega-3 essential fatty acids. The salsa ingredients are outstanding foods for maintaining the immune system.

Sole fillets with parsley sauce

This is a fabulous and elegant dish. All it involves is cooking a fresh fish in a simple way – by poaching – and enhancing its natural flavour with a sauce made from fresh herbs – parsley and coriander.

INGREDIENTS *4 x 175 g (6 oz) sole fillets, cleaned ‖ 2 tablespoons olive oil ‖ 2 tablespoons dry white wine ‖ salt and freshly ground black pepper ‖ plain White Rice (see page 41 – omit the Poblano Chilli Strips), to serve*
SAUCE *3 tablespoons olive oil ‖ 3 garlic cloves, finely diced ‖ 3 tablespoons finely chopped flat leaf parsley leaves ‖ 3 tablespoons finely chopped fresh coriander leaves ‖ 30 g (1 oz) unsalted butter ‖ ½ teaspoon freshly squeezed lime juice ‖ salt and freshly ground black pepper*

ONE Brush the sole fillets with the oil and season with salt and pepper. Place the fillets in a large frying pan and drizzle with the wine. Cover and gently poach over a low heat for 7–10 minutes until cooked through. **TWO** Meanwhile, to make the sauce, heat the oil in a heavy-based saucepan over a medium heat and gently sauté the garlic for 1 minute. Add the parsley and coriander and sauté for about 3 minutes. Add half the butter and season to taste with salt and pepper. Add the lime juice. Keep the sauce warm until ready to serve. Stir in the remaining butter just before serving. **THREE** Transfer the sole fillets to a warm plate and spoon the sauce over the fillets. Serve immediately with the plain White Rice (see page 41).

Serves 4

NUTRIENT ANALYSIS PER SERVING 1370 kJ – 330 kcal – 30 g protein – 0 g carbohydrate – 0 g sugars – 22 g fat – 6 g saturates – 0 g fibre – 176 mg sodium

HEALTHY TIP White fish is an excellent source of protein and also contains minerals and some vitamins; it is low in fat and cholesterol. Parsley is an effective diuretic, useful for kidney disorders. Coriander has antibiotic properties and helps to treat digestive problems. Garlic is highly beneficial for the immune system.

Sea bass in citrus juice

Fresh sea bass is seasoned with garlic and lime rind and then poached in orange juice to give this dish an unexpected and distinctive flavour.

INGREDIENTS *4 x 175 g (6 oz) sea bass fillets, cleaned ‖ 2 garlic cloves, crushed ‖ finely grated rind of 1 lime ‖ 2 tablespoons olive oil ‖ ½ teaspoon salt ‖ freshly squeezed juice of 2 oranges ‖ a few thyme sprigs, plus extra to garnish ‖ freshly ground black pepper ‖ orange slices, to garnish*

ONE Place the fish fillets in a glass bowl. Rub with the garlic, lime rind and oil, and season with the salt and pepper. Cover and leave to marinate in the refrigerator for 1 hour. **TWO** Pour the orange juice into a large heavy-based saucepan, add the thyme sprigs and place the fish fillets on top. Cover and cook over a low heat for 6–8 minutes, or until the fish is cooked through. **THREE** Transfer the fish to a warm serving dish. Reduce the orange sauce by boiling rapidly for a few minutes and pour over the fish. **FOUR** Serve immediately, garnished with the orange slices and extra thyme sprigs.

Serves 4

NUTRIENT ANALYSIS PER SERVING 999 kJ – 238 kcal – 34 g protein – 3 g carbohydrate – 3 g sugars – 10 g fat – 2 g saturates – 0 g fibre – 364 mg sodium

HEALTHY TIP This recipe offers a great combination of healthy ingredients. The oranges have significant antioxidant properties and also stimulate the immune system, liver function and appetite, while the sea bass is a low-fat fish and rich in magnesium, a mineral important for bone health.

Red snapper Veracuz-style

This is one of the most popular dishes in Mexico, traditionally made with red snapper, but equally good with any white fish. The sauce, of international acclaim, is the result of a combination of ingredients from two cultures – pre-Hispanic Mexico and Spain.

INGREDIENTS *4 x 175 g (6 oz) red snapper fillets or white fish fillets, cleaned* ‖ *1 tablespoon freshly squeezed lime juice* ‖ *1 tablespoon olive oil* ‖ *1 onion, finely chopped* ‖ *2 garlic cloves, finely chopped* ‖ *8 large plum tomatoes, skinned, deseeded and finely chopped* ‖ *1 jalapeño chilli, deseeded and finely sliced* ‖ *16 green olives, pitted and sliced* ‖ *1 tablespoon capers* ‖ *1 bay leaf* ‖ *pinch of dried oregano* ‖ *4 Spanish yellow peppers in brine, drained (if available)* ‖ *salt and freshly ground black pepper* ‖ *flat leaf parsley sprigs, to garnish*

ONE Place the fish fillets in a glass bowl. Sprinkle them with the lime juice and season with salt and pepper. Cover and leave to marinate in the refrigerator for 30–45 minutes. **TWO** Heat the oil in a heavy-based frying pan over a medium heat and sauté the onion for about 7 minutes, until soft. Add the garlic and sauté for about a further minute. Add the tomatoes, chilli, olives, capers, bay leaf and oregano and bring to the boil. Reduce the heat and simmer for about 20 minutes, stirring constantly. Season to taste with salt and pepper and leave to cool completely. **THREE** Place the fish fillets in the cold sauce, making sure that the fish is well covered with the sauce. Cover and cook over a low heat for about 6–8 minutes, or until the fish is cooked through. **FOUR** Serve immediately, garnished with the Spanish yellow peppers, if using, and parsley sprigs.

Serves 4

NUTRIENT ANALYSIS PER SERVING 1100 kJ – 264 kcal – 35 g protein – 10 g carbohydrate – 9 g sugars – 9 g fat – 1 g saturates – 4 g fibre – 560 mg sodium

HEALTHY TIP This sauce contains healthy ingredients such as tomatoes, rich in vitamins A and C, and olives, believed to reduce the risk of cardiovascular disease. Olives contain several important vitamins and minerals including vitamins A and E, phosphorus, potassium and manganese.

Seafood casserole

With the thousands of kilometres of coastline surrounding the country, Mexico offers a great variety of delicious fish and shellfish in abundance. You can enjoy them in the different types of regional dishes, which vary according to the customs and the local ingredients. This recipe features an enticing, nutritious mixture, cooked in a fresh tomato sauce.

INGREDIENTS *4 tablespoons olive oil ‖ ½ onion, finely chopped ‖ 4 garlic cloves, crushed ‖ 1 kg (2 lb) tomatoes, skinned, deseeded and chopped ‖ 1 bay leaf ‖ 300 g (10 oz) uncooked king tiger prawns, peeled and deveined ‖ 300 g (10 oz) uncooked king scallops, white part only ‖ 300 g (10 oz) halibut fillet, cut into bite-sized cubes ‖ 300 g (10 oz) uncooked squid, cleaned and cut into thin rings ‖ 300 g (10 oz) cooked octopus, cut into 3 cm (1¼ inch) pieces ‖ 1 tablespoon finely chopped flat leaf parsley ‖ salt and freshly ground black pepper ‖ plain White Rice (see page 41 – omit the Poblano Chilli Strips), to serve*

ONE Heat 2 tablespoons of the oil in a heavy-based saucepan over a medium heat and sauté the onion until soft. Add the garlic and sauté for a further minute. Add the tomatoes and bay leaf and bring to the boil. Reduce the heat and simmer gently for about 20 minutes, stirring constantly. Season to taste with salt and pepper. If the sauce is very thick, add a little water. Keep hot. **TWO** Heat the remaining oil in a wok or a large heavy-based frying pan. Add the prawns, scallops, halibut, squid and octopus, season with salt and pepper and sauté over a high heat for 2–3 minutes. Add the hot sauce and bring to the boil briefly. Check the seasoning. **THREE** Transfer to a hot serving platter and sprinkle the parsley on top. Serve immediately with the plain White Rice (see page 41).

Serves 4

NUTRIENT ANALYSIS PER SERVING 1876 kJ – 445 kcal – 61 g protein – 13 g carbohydrate – 8 g sugars – 17 g fat – 3 g saturates – 4 g fibre – 754 mg sodium

HEALTHY TIP Shellfish are an excellent source of protein; they are low in fat and rich in essential minerals such as zinc, selenium and copper. They also are a good source of vitamin B12 and niacin.

Halibut fillets with dried chilli sauce

Enjoy the texture and flavour of halibut fillets, cooked in a lavish chilli sauce made with a combination of three varieties of earthy and fruity dried chillies.

INGREDIENTS *4 x 175 g (6 oz) halibut fillets or other white fish, skinned and cleaned* ‖ *2 tablespoons olive oil* ‖ *1½ tablespoons freshly squeezed lime juice* ‖ *2 ancho chillies* ‖ *2 mulato chillies* ‖ *2 guajillo chillies* ‖ *4 garlic cloves, finely chopped* ‖ *250 ml (8 fl oz) dry white wine* ‖ *a few drops of Worcestershire sauce* ‖ *salt and freshly ground black pepper* ‖ *1 flat leaf parsley sprig, to garnish*

ONE Place the fish fillets in a glass bowl. Rub with 1 tablespoon of the oil, sprinkle with ½ tablespoon of the lime juice and season with salt and pepper. Cover and leave to marinate in the refrigerator for 15–20 minutes. **TWO** Remove the stems from the chillies, discard the seeds and cut into thin rings. **THREE** Heat the remaining oil in a heavy-based frying pan over a medium heat and sauté the garlic for 1 minute. Add the chillies and sauté for a further minute. Add the remaining lime juice, wine and Worcestershire sauce and gently simmer for about 5 minutes. Season the sauce to taste with salt and pepper and leave to cool completely. **FOUR** Place the fish fillets in the cold sauce, taking care that the fish is well covered with the sauce. Cover and gently simmer over a low heat for about 8 minutes, or until cooked through. **FIVE** Serve immediately, covering the fillets with the sauce, and garnished with the parsley sprig.

Serves 4

NUTRIENT ANALYSIS PER SERVING 1108 kJ – 264 kcal – 32 g protein – 2 g carbohydrate – 2 g sugars – 10 g fat – 1 g saturates – 0 g fibre – 168 mg sodium

HEALTHY TIP Fish is one of the healthiest foods, rich in proteins, minerals and vitamins, and low in fat in comparison with meat. Poaching the fish in the sauce not only keeps its flavour but helps to retain the rich nutrients.

Cod fillet in tomatillo sauce

This flavoursome dish is cooked in one of Mexico's favourite sauces, made with tomatillos, a fruit that resembles a small tomato except that it is green and covered with a thin papery husk. Choose firm fruit with a dry, tight-fitting husk, and remove the husk before using.

INGREDIENTS *1 x 750 g (1½ lb) cod fillet* ‖ *1 tablespoon olive oil* ‖ *1 garlic clove, crushed* ‖ *freshly squeezed juice of ½ lime* ‖ *salt and freshly ground black pepper*

SALSA VERDE *225 g (7½ oz) tomatillos, husks removed* ‖ *30 g (1 oz) fresh coriander* ‖ *30 g (1 oz) onion* ‖ *2 jalapeño chillies* ‖ *4 salad onions, diagonally sliced, to garnish*

ONE Put the cod fillet in a glass bowl. Rub with the oil and garlic, season with salt and pepper and drizzle the lime juice on top. Cover and set aside. **TWO** Blend all the salsa ingredients together in a blender or food processor. **THREE** Place the cod fillet in a large heavy-based frying pan. Pour over the salsa, cover and gently poach over a low heat for 7–10 minutes until cooked through. **FOUR** Transfer the cod fillet to a warm serving plate, pour the sauce over and garnish with the sliced onions and serve immediately.

Serves 4

NUTRIENT ANALYSIS PER SERVING 778 kJ – 184 kcal – 34 g protein – 3 g carbohydrate – 3 g sugars – 4 g fat – 1 g saturates – 1 g fibre – 150 mg sodium

HEALTHY TIP White fish is one of the most nutritionally balanced foods. Cod in particular promotes cardiovascular health because of its low fat content. The fat in cod is a good source of blood-thinning omega-3 fatty acids. (If possible, try to use cod from sustainable sources or farmed cod.) Tomatillo salsa contains ingredients rich in vitamins A and C, and also provides dietary fibre.

Rainbow trout in papillotte

In this dish, rainbow trout are rubbed with lime juice and stuffed with a mixture of onion, chilli, garlic and fresh coriander, where the chillies give a really distinctive edge, creating a harmony of flavours and textures.

INGREDIENTS *4 rainbow trout, cleaned and gutted* ‖ *2 tablespoons freshly squeezed lime juice* ‖ *salt and freshly ground black pepper* ‖ *1 tablespoon olive oil, plus extra for brushing and oiling* ‖ *½ onion, finely chopped* ‖ *2 garlic cloves, finely chopped* ‖ *2 green chillies, finely sliced* ‖ *2 red chillies, finely sliced* ‖ *large bunch of fresh coriander, chopped*

ONE Rinse the fish and pat dry. With a sharp knife, cut 3 diagonal slashes in the sides of the each fish. Rub the fish inside and out with the lime juice and season with salt and pepper. **TWO** Heat the oil in a frying pan over a gentle heat and sauté the onion for about 7 minutes until translucent. Add the garlic and chillies and sauté for a further minute. Transfer to a bowl and leave to cool. Add the coriander and season to taste with salt and pepper. **THREE** Divide the coriander mixture into quarters and use each quarter to stuff a trout, rubbing some of the mixture inside the slashes in the sides of the fish. **FOUR** Cut 4 x 30 cm (12 inch) squares of greaseproof paper. Brush one side of each paper square with a little oil, leaving the edges free. Place each trout on one half of the oiled side of a paper square. Fold the paper over the fish and twist the side edges together, pressing hard to seal and form a parcel (papillotte). **FIVE** Place the papillottes on a lightly oiled baking sheet and bake in a preheated oven, 200°C (400°F), Gas Mark 6, for 18–20 minutes until the fish is cooked. **SIX** Serve immediately, allowing each diner to open their own papillotte at the table.

Serves 4

NUTRIENT ANALYSIS PER SERVING 1155 kJ – 275 kcal – 37 g protein – 1 g carbohydrate – 1 g sugars – 14 g fat – 3 g saturates – 0 g fibre – 96 mg sodium

HEALTHY TIP Trout, which is high in omega-3 polyunsaturated fatty acids, can cut the risk of heart attacks by lowering blood fat levels and reducing blood clotting. It is an excellent source of vitamins and minerals, and also contains natural oils that help to keep the skin and hair in good condition. It is recommended to eat at least one portion of oily fish a week.

Tiger prawn brochettes with ajillo oil

Prawns are a favourite shellfish of Mexicans. They abound in the Gulf of Mexico as well as on the Pacific Coast, and are used to prepare many regional dishes. This combination of garlic and *guajillo* chilli, fried in olive oil – *ajillo* – is traditionally served in restaurants in the central regions of the country.

INGREDIENTS *20 uncooked king tiger prawns, in their shells (with heads intact)*

MARINADE *¼ onion, chopped ‖ 1–2 garlic cloves, chopped ‖ 2 tablespoons olive oil ‖ salt and freshly ground black pepper*

AJILLO OIL *2 guajillo chillies ‖ 4 tablespoons olive oil ‖ 5 garlic cloves, peeled but kept whole*

ONE Peel the prawns, keeping the heads and tails on (for presentation purposes). Make a small cut down the centre of the back of each prawn and carefully remove the black vein. Rinse and pat dry. **TWO** Purée the marinade ingredients in a blender or food processor. Spread the marinade over the prawns, cover and leave to marinate in the refrigerator for at least 30 minutes. **THREE** To make the ajillo oil, cut the chillies into thin rings, discarding the seeds. Heat the oil in a small saucepan over a medium heat and gently sauté the garlic cloves until golden brown. Add the chilli rings and quickly sauté for a few seconds, then remove from the heat, stir and leave to infuse for at least 15 minutes. Transfer to a serving bowl and keep at room temperature. **FOUR** Preheat the grill to medium-high. Thread the prawns on to metal skewers and cook the brochettes under the grill for 2–3 minutes, turning halfway through, until the prawns are cooked – they are ready when they have turned pink and curled up. **FIVE** Place the brochettes on a warm serving plate, sprinkle with the *ajillo* oil and serve immediately.

Serves 4

NUTRIENT ANALYSIS PER SERVING 805 kJ – 195 kcal – 9 g protein – 1 g carbohydrate – 1 g sugars – 17 g fat – 2 g saturates – 0 g fibre – 96 mg sodium

HEALTHY TIP Prawns are naturally low in saturated fat. They are an excellent source of protein and also contain a number of essential nutrients, such as magnesium, which plays a role in bone development and nerve and muscle function, zinc, which is good for growth, and selenium, an important antioxidant. Garlic is well known for its antibacterial, antioxidant and antiseptic properties.

Poultry and eggs

Huevos rancheros

In this internationally famed dish, fried eggs are placed over a corn tortilla, then covered with a delicious tomato sauce. This is a classic item of the Mexican breakfast menu and is traditionally served with black beans and extra tortillas or crusty white bread to mop up every bit of the delicious sauce.

INGREDIENTS *4 soft corn tortillas* ‖ *vegetable oil, for brushing* ‖ *8 large organic free-range eggs*

RANCHERA SAUCE *4 medium-large ripe tomatoes* ‖ *½ onion, roughly chopped* ‖ *1 garlic clove, roughly chopped* ‖ *4 green chillies, roughly chopped (deseeded for a milder taste)* ‖ *1 tablespoon vegetable oil* ‖ *salt* ‖ *chopped flat leaf parsley, to garnish (optional)*

ONE First make the sauce. Put the tomatoes, onion, garlic and chillies in a blender or food processor and blend to a fairly smooth texture. **TWO** Heat the oil in a medium saucepan over a medium heat, add the tomato mixture and simmer for about 10 minutes, or until cooked, stirring constantly. Add salt to taste and keep warm until required. **THREE** Preheat a large, dry heavy-based frying pan over a medium heat. Brush the tortillas with oil and warm each side of 2–3 tortillas at a time in the hot pan for about 30 seconds until soft. Cover with foil to keep warm. **FOUR** Preheat a dry non-stick frying pan over a medium heat. Break the eggs, 2 at a time, into the pan and cook over a low heat until the whites have set. **FIVE** Put one tortilla on each plate and place 2 cooked eggs on top. Spoon the ranchera sauce generously over the whites of the eggs, leaving the yolks exposed, and serve immediately with flat leaf parsley scattered over the top, if liked.

Serves 4

NUTRIENT ANALYSIS PER SERVING 1485 kJ – 355 kcal – 19 g protein – 26 g carbohydrate – 3 g sugars – 19 g fat – 4 g saturates – 2 g fibre – 275 mg sodium

HEALTHY TIP To reduce the amount of oil traditionally used in this dish, in this recipe the eggs are cooked in a dry non-stick frying pan, and the tortillas are brushed with a little oil instead of being deep-fried.

Scrambled eggs Mexican-style

These delicious scrambled eggs with chopped tomato, onion and green chilli are known as 'a la mexicana' because the colours of these last three ingredients echo the colours of the Mexican flag. This is a typical breakfast dish and combines naturally with warm soft corn tortillas, beans and any Mexican salsa.

INGREDIENTS *1½ tablespoons vegetable oil* ‖ *½ onion, finely chopped* ‖ *8 large organic free-range eggs, beaten* ‖ *3 plum tomatoes, skinned, deseeded and finely chopped* ‖ *2 green chillies, chopped (deseeded for a milder taste)* ‖ *salt*

ONE Heat the oil in a large heavy-based frying pan and gently sauté the onion until soft. **TWO** Pour in the beaten eggs, chopped tomatoes and chillies. Season with salt. Gently stir the egg mixture over the heat until set to your taste. **THREE** Place on a warm dish and serve immediately.

Serves 4

NUTRIENT ANALYSIS PER SERVING 900 kJ – 217 kcal – 15 g protein – 3 g carbohydrate – 3 g sugars – 16 g fat – 4 g saturates – 1 g fibre – 164 mg sodium

HEALTHY TIP Scrambling the eggs helps to break down their protein, making them much easier to digest. However, if you are concerned about your cholesterol level, try this recipe using the whites only – they provide more than half of the eggs' protein, potassium and riboflavin, and contain no cholesterol.

'Divorced' eggs

This speciality dish for breakfast in Mexico City, similar to Huevos Rancheros (see page 74), consists of two fried eggs placed over fried corn tortillas and covered with a red sauce over one egg and green sauce over the other. It is commonly served with black beans.

INGREDIENTS *4 soft corn tortillas* ‖ *vegetable oil, for brushing* ‖ *8 large organic free-range eggs*

RED SAUCE *4 medium-large ripe tomatoes* ‖ *½ onion, roughly chopped* ‖ *1 garlic clove, roughly chopped* ‖ *4 green chillies, roughly chopped* ‖ *1 tablespoon vegetable oil* ‖ *salt*

GREEN SAUCE *225 g (7½ oz) tomatillos, husks removed* ‖ *30 g (1 oz) fresh coriander* ‖ *30 g (1 oz) onion* ‖ *2 green chillies (deseeded for a milder taste)* ‖ *salt*

ONE To make the red sauce, put the tomatoes, onion, garlic and chillies in a blender or food processor and blend to a fairly smooth texture. Heat the oil in a medium saucepan over a medium heat, add the tomato mixture and cook for about 10 minutes, or until cooked, stirring constantly. Season to taste with salt and keep warm until required. **TWO** Purée all the green sauce ingredients in a blender or food processor. Heat the tomatillo mixture in a medium saucepan over a medium heat, season to taste with salt and keep warm until required. **THREE** Preheat a large, dry heavy-based frying pan over a medium heat. Brush the tortillas with oil and warm each side of 2–3 tortillas at a time in the hot pan for about 30 seconds until soft. Cover with foil to keep warm. **FOUR** Preheat a dry non-stick frying pan over a medium heat. Break the eggs, 2 at a time, into the pan and cook over a low heat until the whites have set. **FIVE** Put one tortilla on each plate and place 2 cooked eggs on top. Spoon red sauce generously over the white of one of the eggs, leaving the yolk exposed, then spoon green sauce generously over the white of the other egg. Repeat with the remaining eggs. Serve immediately.

Serves 4

NUTRIENT ANALYSIS PER SERVING 1455 kJ – 346 kcal – 20 g protein – 30 g carbohydrate – 6 g sugars – 17 g fat – 4 g saturates – 4 g fibre – 280 mg sodium

HEALTHY TIP This is a healthy, nutritious dish for breakfast, rich in vitamins, minerals and high-quality protein from the eggs. The ingredients used for the sauces are also a good source of dietary fibre. Using a dry, non-stick frying pan to cook the eggs minimizes the oil content of the dish.

'Rabo de mestiza' poached eggs

This colourful dish is an exciting blend of textures and flavours where the eggs are poached in a tomato sauce with poblano chilli strips and garnished with fresh white cheese – sometimes topped with a generous dollop of cream. It is commonly eaten as a main course during Lent.

INGREDIENTS *2 poblano chillies* ‖ *750 g (1½ lb) ripe tomatoes* ‖ *1 onion, roughly chopped* ‖ *2 garlic cloves, roughly chopped* ‖ *500 ml (17 fl oz) chicken stock* ‖ *1½ tablespoons vegetable oil* ‖ *1 bay leaf* ‖ *8 large organic free-range eggs* ‖ *50 g (2 oz) mozzarella cheese, cut into julienne strips* ‖ *salt* ‖ *chopped fresh coriander leaves, to garnish* ‖ *warm soft corn tortillas, to serve*

ONE Carefully hold the chillies over a high gas flame with metal kitchen tongs or put in a preheated dry heavy-based frying pan over a high heat, turning frequently, until the skins are charred. Put the roasted chillies in a plastic bag, wrap the bag with a tea towel and leave to sweat for at least 15 minutes. Remove the skins, rinse the chillies under cold running water and discard the stems and seeds. Pat dry and slice lengthways into strips. **TWO** Put the tomatoes, onion, garlic and half the stock in a blender or food processor and blend to a fairly smooth texture. Pass the mixture through a sieve. **THREE** Heat the oil in a heavy-based saucepan (25 cm/10 inches in diameter) over a medium heat, add the tomato mixture and bay leaf and gently simmer for 15–20 minutes until cooked, stirring occasionally. Add the poblano strips and, if the sauce is too thick, add some more of the remaining stock. Bring to the boil and season to taste with salt. **FOUR** Break the eggs, one at a time, into the sauce, cover and cook over a gently heat for a few minutes until the whites have set. Just before removing from the heat, add the mozzarella. **FIVE** Serve immediately, garnished with coriander and accompanied by warm corn tortillas.

Serves 4

NUTRIENT ANALYSIS PER SERVING 1187 kJ – 284 kcal – 19 g protein – 8 g carbohydrate – 7 g sugars – 20 g fat – 6 g saturates – 3 g fibre – 456 mg sodium

HEALTHY TIP Eggs are a good source of high-quality protein, low in fat and rich in vitamin A, and also contain many of the B group vitamins and minerals. In addition, tomatoes are an excellent source of antioxidants, including vitamins A and C, and they also contain potassium and dietary fibre.

Green bean omelette with pasilla chilli sauce

This is a favourite way of enjoying eggs and fresh green beans. The pasilla chilli sauce adds an elegant touch to the omelette. It makes a tasty and nutritious lunch, served with a healthy salad and crusty bread.

INGREDIENTS *65 g (2½ oz) green beans* ‖ *8 large organic free-range eggs* ‖ *4 teaspoons unsalted butter* ‖ *salt and freshly ground black pepper* ‖ *flat leaf parsley, to garnish* ‖ *warm tortillas, to serve*
PASILLA CHILLI SAUCE *4 pasilla chillies* ‖ *¼ onion* ‖ *1 garlic clove, unpeeled* ‖ *1 teaspoon vegetable oil* ‖ *salt*

ONE First make the sauce. Remove the stems from the chillies, tear the chillies open and remove the seeds (for a milder sauce, remove all the stringy, light-coloured veins as well). Heat a dry heavy-based frying pan over a medium heat and lightly roast for a few seconds on both sides. Transfer to a heatproof bowl, cover with boiling water and leave to soak for 15–20 minutes until soft. **TWO** Put the onion and garlic clove on the hot surface of the frying pan and cook, turning occasionally, until soft. Leave to cool, then peel the garlic. **THREE** Drain the chillies and transfer to a blender or food processor with some of their soaking water, add the onion and garlic and blend until smooth. Pass the mixture through a sieve. **FOUR** Heat the oil in a heavy-based saucepan over a medium heat, add the chilli mixture and gently simmer for about 15 minutes until cooked. Season to taste with salt. Keep warm until required. **FIVE** Meanwhile, steam the green beans for 5–10 minutes, depending on thickness, until just tender, cut them into 1 cm (½ inch) pieces and set aside. **SIX** Break 2 eggs into a bowl and whisk with a fork until frothy. Season with salt and pepper. Heat 1 teaspoon of the butter in an omelette pan. When sizzling, pour in the eggs and cook over a medium heat, gently stirring, until the bottom has set and the top is still creamy. Sprinkle over a quarter of the green beans, fold in half and transfer to a warm dish. Pour some of the sauce on top. Repeat with the remaining butter, eggs and beans. **SEVEN** Serve immediately with warm tortillas and flat leaf parsley scattered over the top.

Serves 4

NUTRIENT ANALYSIS PER SERVING 955 kJ – 230 kcal – 15 g protein – 1 g carbohydrate – 1 g sugars – 18 g fat – 7 g saturates – 1 g fibre – 166 mg sodium

HEALTHY TIP If you are concerned with your fat intake, use a non-stick omelette pan and reduce the amount of butter even further. Green beans are low in calories and rich in nutrients such as vitamin C, vitamin K, manganese and dietary fibre, among others. Steaming them helps to retain their nutrients.

Chicken breast with pine nut sauce

Sauces made with nuts such as pine nuts and almonds are an ideal companion to chicken dishes. This elegant and delicate sauce made with ground pine nuts and a hint of chilli has an attractive creamy colour and is prepared for special occasions.

INGREDIENTS *4 x 175 g (6 oz) boneless, skinless chicken breasts* ‖ *1 red chilli, deseeded and cut lengthways into thin strips, to garnish*

MARINADE *finely grated rind and freshly squeezed juice of 1 lime* ‖ *1 tablespoon vegetable oil* ‖ *salt and freshly ground black pepper*

SAUCE *1 tablespoon vegetable oil* ‖ *1 small onion, finely chopped* ‖ *2 garlic cloves, finely chopped* ‖ *3 red chillies, deseeded and finely chopped* ‖ *175 g (6 oz) pine nuts, plus 25 g (1 oz), lightly toasted, to garnish* ‖ *250 ml (8 fl oz) chicken stock* ‖ *salt and white pepper*

ONE Mix the marinade ingredients together in a glass bowl, add the chicken and mix together well. Cover and leave to marinate overnight in the refrigerator. **TWO** Transfer the chicken and marinade to an ovenproof dish, cover with foil and cook in a preheated oven, 200°C (400°F), Gas Mark 6, for about 30 minutes, or until cooked through. Leave to rest for 10 minutes before serving. **THREE** Meanwhile, make the sauce. Heat the oil in a heavy-based saucepan and sauté the onion until translucent. Add the garlic and chillies and sauté for a further minute. **FOUR** Transfer the onion mixture to a blender or food processor with the pine nuts and stock and blend until smooth. **FIVE** Pour the pine nut mixture into a saucepan and cook over a medium heat for 10 minutes, stirring occasionally. If the sauce gets too thick, add more stock. Season to taste with salt and pepper. **SIX** Cut each chicken breast into 4 and arrange on individual plates. Pour the sauce over the chicken, garnish with the toasted pine nuts and strips of chilli and serve immediately.

Serves 4

NUTRIENT ANALYSIS PER SERVING 2535 kJ – 610 kcal – 46 g protein – 4 g carbohydrate – 3 g sugars – 46 g fat – 5 g saturates – 2 g fibre – 330 mg sodium

HEALTHY TIP Chicken is a very good source of protein and niacin, a cancer-protective B vitamin, and also selenium, essential to human health. Pine nuts are good source of dietary fibre.

Chicken in tomatillo and chipotle chilli sauce

This family dish is customarily made with pork or chicken meat, together with tomatillos and chipotle chillies. It is mainly eaten at lunchtime and makes a good main course served with plain white rice, beans and warm corn tortillas.

INGREDIENTS *4 x 175 g (6 oz) boneless, skinless chicken breasts* ‖ *2 tablespoons vegetable oil* ‖ *1 onion, finely chopped* ‖ *2 garlic cloves, crushed* ‖ *625 g (1¼ lb) chopped fresh tomatillos, husks removed* ‖ *2 chipotle chillies, bottled or canned in adobo sauce, chopped* ‖ *1 teaspoon soft light brown sugar* ‖ *1 teaspoon dried oregano, or to taste* ‖ *200 ml (7 fl oz) chicken stock* ‖ *salt and freshly ground black pepper*

ONE Trim any fat from the chicken breasts and season with salt and pepper. Heat 1 tablespoon of the oil in a heavy-based saucepan over a medium heat and lightly brown the chicken breasts on both sides. Remove to a plate. **TWO** Add the remaining oil, heat over a medium heat and sauté the onion until soft. Add the garlic, tomatillos and chillies and sauté for a further 5 minutes. Add the sugar, oregano and stock, and simmer for 2 minutes. Season to taste with salt and pepper. **THREE** Place the chicken breasts in the sauce, cover and gently simmer for 25–30 minutes until cooked through. Serve hot.

Serves 4

NUTRIENT ANALYSIS PER SERVING 1260 kJ – 300 kcal – 40 g protein – 9 g carbohydrate – 8 g sugars – 12 g fat – 3 g saturates – 3 g fibre – 158 mg sodium

HEALTHY TIP Chicken is best skinned before cooking, as leaving the skin on doubles the amount of fat. The breast is the leanest part of the chicken.

Chicken mixiotes in almond and chilli sauce

Mixiote is the tough outer skin of the maguey, a plant belonging to the succulent family. It was traditionally used to wrap bite-sized portions of marinated meat with sauce into small parcels, tied with string. Nowadays, it is common to use greaseproof paper instead of maguey skin to prepare this dish.

INGREDIENTS *4 x 175 g (6 oz) boneless, skinless chicken breasts, diced* ‖ *warm soft corn tortillas, to serve*

SAUCE *3 ancho chillies* ‖ *1 tomato* ‖ *¼ onion, roughly chopped* ‖ *2 garlic cloves, unpeeled* ‖ *200 ml (7 fl oz) chicken stock* ‖ *1 tablespoon vegetable oil* ‖ *50 g (2 oz) almonds with skins on, ground* ‖ *¼ teaspoon dried oregano* ‖ *pinch of dried thyme* ‖ *salt*

ONE First make the sauce. Remove the stems from the chillies, tear the chillies open and remove the seeds (for a milder sauce, remove all the stringy, light-coloured veins as well). Heat a dry heavy-based frying pan over a medium heat and lightly roast the chillies for a few seconds on both sides. Transfer to a heatproof bowl, cover with boiling water and leave to soak for 15–20 minutes until soft. **TWO** Meanwhile, put the tomato, onion and garlic cloves on the hot surface of the frying pan and roast, turning occasionally, until soft. Leave to cool, then peel the garlic. **THREE** Drain the chillies and transfer to a blender or food processor. Add the tomato, onion, garlic and the stock and blend until smooth. Pass the mixture through a sieve. **FOUR** Heat the oil in a heavy-based saucepan, add the chilli mixture, almonds and herbs and simmer for about 15 minutes, stirring constantly, until the sauce is cooked. Season to taste with salt and leave to cool completely. **FIVE** Put the chicken in a glass bowl, add the sauce and mix together well. Cover and leave to marinate in the refrigerator for at least 2 hours. **SIX** Cut 4 x 24 cm (9½ inch) squares of greaseproof paper. Place a quarter of the chicken mixture in the centre of each square, pull up the sides and make 4 parcels. Tie securely with string. **SEVEN** Place the parcels in an ovenproof dish inside a large roasting tin half-filled with hot water, making sure that the water does not touch the parcels. Steam-bake in a preheated oven, 180°C (350°F), Gas Mark 4, for 50 minutes until the chicken is cooked through and tender. **EIGHT** Serve hot, letting each diner untie their own mixiote, with warm corn tortillas.

Serves 4

NUTRIENT ANALYSIS PER SERVING 1330 kJ – 317 kcal – 42 g protein – 3 g carbohydrate – 2 g sugars – 16 g fat – 3 g saturates – 2 g fibre – 335 mg sodium

HEALTHY TIP Steaming is the healthiest cooking method, as fewer nutrients are lost or destroyed. Flavours and textures also remain more intact than with frying or boiling in water.

Turkey with Xico-style mole sauce

This mole (from the Nahuatl word *Molli*, meaning sauce) is from Xico in the state of Veracruz. Prepare the mole paste in advance and let the flavour develop.

INGREDIENTS *1 x 2–3 kg (4–6½ lb) whole turkey breast, halved* ‖ *1 onion* ‖ *4 garlic cloves, peeled but kept whole* ‖ *plain White Rice (see page 41 – omit the Poblano Chilli Strips), to serve* ‖ *chopped flat leaf parsley, to garnish (optional)*

MOLE SAUCE *125 g (4 oz) mulato chillies* ‖ *40 g (1½ oz) pasilla chillies* ‖ *20 g (¾ oz) ancho chillies* ‖ *½ large onion, chopped* ‖ *3 garlic cloves, peeled but kept whole* ‖ *300 g (10 oz) tomatoes* ‖ *5 tablespoons vegetable oil* ‖ *2 soft corn tortillas* ‖ *1 petit pain* ‖ *75 g (3 oz) pitted prunes* ‖ *30 g (1 oz) raisins* ‖ *¼ plantain* ‖ *25 g (1 oz) blanched almonds, toasted* ‖ *25 g (1 oz) blanched hazelnuts, toasted* ‖ *25 g (1 oz) pine nuts, toasted* ‖ *25 g (1 oz) sesame seeds, toasted, plus 1 tablespoon to garnish* ‖ *25 g (1 oz) walnuts, toasted* ‖ *¼ teaspoon aniseed* ‖ *½ cinnamon stick, broken and toasted* ‖ *2 whole cloves, toasted* ‖ *3 allspice berries, toasted* ‖ *5 black peppercorns, toasted* ‖ *40 g (1½ oz) soft light brown sugar* ‖ *salt*

ONE Put the turkey, onion and garlic cloves in a saucepan, cover with water and bring to the boil. Simmer for 1–1½ hours until cooked, skimming off any scum. Lift out the turkey, strain the broth and leave to cool. Refrigerate until required. **TWO** Remove the stems from the chillies, tear the chillies open and remove the seeds, then roast for a few seconds on both sides in a hot frying pan. Soak them in boiling water for 20 minutes until soft. **THREE** Roast the onion, garlic cloves and tomatoes in the frying pan until soft. **FOUR** Transfer the chillies with some of their soaking water, onion, garlic and tomatoes to a blender or food processor and blend to a smooth texture, then sieve. **FIVE** Heat half of the oil in a saucepan, pour in the chilli mixture and simmer for about 20 minutes, stirring occasionally. **SIX** Heat the remaining oil in a frying pan and, one at a time, briefly sauté the tortillas, bread, prunes, raisins and plantain. Blend these with some of the chilli mixture to a smooth texture. Add to the remaining chilli mixture. **SEVEN** Grind the nuts, seeds and spices, add to the sauce and simmer for about 45 minutes, stirring constantly until it is a thick paste. Add some turkey broth to adjust the consistency. Add the sugar and salt to taste. **EIGHT** Slice the turkey, add to the sauce and simmer for 10 minutes. Serve the turkey with the sauce spooned over and garnished with sesame seeds and flat leaf parsley, if liked, with the White Rice.

Serves 8

NUTRIENT ANALYSIS PER SERVING 2216 kJ – 530 kcal – 44 g protein – 27 g carbohydrate – 15 g sugars – 28 g fat – 5 g saturates – 4 g fibre – 204 mg sodium

HEALTHY TIP The turkey is a good source of proteins and some B vitamins.

Duck tacos

Duck was eaten in Mexico before the arrival of the Spanish. It is mainly consumed in the southern states of the country. Duck tacos are a traditional dish, typically served with a very hot sauce in Mexico City bars where workers go to drink, eat and even play a few rounds of dominoes.

INGREDIENTS *1 x 1.75 kg (3½ lb) hot roasted duck* ‖ *16 soft corn tortillas* ‖ *1 onion, finely chopped* ‖ *8 green chillies, chopped (deseeded for a milder taste)* ‖ *30 g (1 oz) fresh coriander, finely chopped* ‖ *salt* ‖ *finely chopped tomato, to garnish (optional)* ‖ *salsa of your choice, to serve*

ONE Shred the duck meat, discard any fat and keep warm. **TWO** Preheat a large, dry heavy-based frying pan over a medium heat. Warm each side of the tortillas, 2–3 at a time, for about 30 seconds in the hot pan until soft. Transfer to a basket and cover with a clean tea towel. **THREE** Put about 20 g (¾ oz) of shredded duck on top of one warm tortilla, scatter some of the onion, chillies and coriander on top, add salt to taste, roll up and place on a warm platter. Cover with the clean tea towel. Repeat with the remaining ingredients. **FOUR** Serve immediately with your favourite salsa and garnish with the chopped tomato, if liked.

Serves 4

NUTRIENT ANALYSIS PER SERVING (using 16 x 40 g (1½ oz tortillas) 3430 kJ – 816 kcal – 54 g protein – 93 g carbohydrate – 2 g sugars – 25 g fat – 4 g saturates – 5 g fibre – 570 mg sodium

HEALTHY TIP Duck can be high in fat, so always remove the skin and as much fat as possible to make this nutritious dish healthier.

Beef brochettes with salsa mexicana

The colours of the ingredients of salsa mexicana are those of the Mexican flag: green, white and red, from the chillies and coriander, onions and tomatoes. Its vibrant flavour matches its visual impact, and makes a healthful accompaniment to these succulent brochettes.

INGREDIENTS *500 g (1 lb) beef fillet* ‖ *1 red onion* ‖ *2 green peppers* ‖ *olive oil, for brushing* ‖ *salt and freshly ground black pepper*

SALSA MEXICANA *4 large ripe tomatoes, skinned, deseeded and finely chopped* ‖ *½ onion, finely chopped* ‖ *3 green chillies, finely chopped* ‖ *2 tablespoons finely chopped fresh coriander* ‖ *1 teaspoon freshly squeezed lime juice (optional)* ‖ *1 tablespoon extra virgin olive oil (optional)* ‖ *salt*

ONE Soak 4 bamboo skewers in cold water for 30 minutes. To make the salsa, mix together the tomatoes, onion, chillies and coriander, add the lime juice and oil, if using, and season to taste with salt. Transfer to a serving bowl and keep at room temperature. **TWO** Cut the beef into 16 bite-sized cubes. Cut the red onion and green peppers into 2.5 cm (1 inch) squares. Thread the beef cubes on to the bamboo skewers, alternating with the onion and green peppers. Brush the brochettes with oil and season with salt and pepper just before cooking. **THREE** Cook the brochettes under a preheated high grill for 4–5 minutes, turning halfway, until the meat is cooked according to your taste. **FOUR** Serve the brochettes with the salsa mexicana on the side.

Serves 4

NUTRIENT ANALYSIS PER SERVING 924 kJ – 219 kcal – 28 g protein – 10 g carbohydrate – 9 g sugars – 8 g fat – 3 g saturates – 4 g fibre – 95 mg sodium

HEALTHY TIP Tomatoes are rich in vitamin C and also contain vitamins A and B, potassium, iron and phosphorous. A medium tomato has almost as much fibre as a slice of wholemeal bread and only about 35 calories.

Meatballs in chipotle sauce

This dish of spicy meatballs – *albondigas* – cooked in a tomato and chipotle chilli sauce is a well-loved one in the central regions of the country and is served at lunchtime at home as well as in restaurants and bars. It is a very popular take-away dish in many markets.

INGREDIENTS *250 g (8 oz) lean minced pork* ‖ *250 g (8 oz) lean minced beef* ‖ *½ small onion, finely chopped* ‖ *1 garlic clove, crushed* ‖ *1 organic free-range egg* ‖ *salt and freshly ground black pepper*

CHIPOTLE SAUCE *3 chipotle chillies* ‖ *1 kg (2 lb) tomatoes* ‖ *½ small onion* ‖ *1 garlic clove, peeled but kept whole* ‖ *1 tablespoon vegetable oil* ‖ *1 bay leaf* ‖ *1 thyme sprig* ‖ *salt*

TO SERVE *plain White Rice (see page 41 – omit the Poblano Chilli Strips)* ‖ *warm soft corn tortillas* ‖ *chopped flat leaf parsley (optional)*

ONE First make the sauce. Remove the stems from the chillies, tear the chillies open and remove the seeds (for a milder sauce, remove all the stringy, light-coloured veins as well). Heat a dry heavy-based frying pan over a medium heat and lightly roast the chillies for a few seconds on both sides. Transfer to a heatproof bowl, cover with boiling water and leave to soak for 15–20 minutes until soft. **TWO** Meanwhile, put the tomatoes, onion and garlic clove on the hot surface of the frying pan and roast, turning occasionally, until soft. **THREE** Drain the chillies and transfer to a blender or food processor. Add the tomatoes, onion and garlic and blend to a fairly smooth texture, adding a little of the chilli soaking water if necessary. Pass through a sieve. **FOUR** Heat the oil in a heavy-based saucepan over a medium heat, add the sauce and gently simmer with the bay leaf and thyme sprig for about 15 minutes until cooked. Season to taste with salt. **FIVE** Meanwhile, to make the meatballs, mix the minced meats, onion, garlic, egg and salt and pepper together in a bowl – for the best result, wear rubber gloves and use your hands. Shape the mixture into chestnut-sized balls. When the sauce is cooked, add the meatballs and bring to the boil. Reduce the heat, cover and gently simmer for about 35 minutes until cooked through and tender. **SIX** Serve immediately with the plain White Rice (see page 41) and warm corn tortillas, with the parsley sprinkled over the top, if liked.

Serves 4

NUTRIENT ANALYSIS PER SERVING 1115 kJ – 266 kcal – 30 g protein – 9 g carbohydrate – 9 g sugars – 12 g fat – 4 g saturates – 4 g fibre – 129 mg sodium

HEALTHY TIP Besides being delicious, meat has a very high nutritional value. Choose the leanest cuts of meat and ask your butcher to mince them.

Meatloaf

Albondigón is the name given to this popular Mexican meatloaf, shaped into a big roll. There are many variations on the recipe, both traditional and contemporary, using different cooking techniques and seasonings. Depending on the region, it could be wrapped in banana leaf, cheesecloth or foil, and can be steamed, baked in a bain-marie or poached. It can also be served either hot or at room temperature.

INGREDIENTS *300 g (10 oz) lean minced veal* ‖ *300 g (10 oz) lean minced beef* ‖ *1 tablespoon finely diced green pepper* ‖ *1 tablespoon finely diced red pepper* ‖ *3 salad onions, finely sliced* ‖ *1–2 garlic cloves, crushed* ‖ *1 large organic free-range egg* ‖ *a few drops of Worcestershire sauce* ‖ *salt and freshly ground black pepper* ‖ *Baby Spinach and Mushroom Salad (see page 120), to serve*

ONE Mix all the ingredients together in a bowl – for the best result, wear rubber gloves and use your hands. Put the meat mixture on a sheet of foil 50 cm (20 inches) long, shape into a big roll and wrap in the foil. **TWO** Transfer the meat roll to a roasting tin, add hot water to come halfway up the sides of the roll and bake in a preheated oven, 180°C (350°F), Gas Mark 4, for about 40 minutes until cooked through. **THREE** Remove the foil and slice the meat on the diagonal. Serve immediately with Baby Spinach and Mushroom Salad (see page 120).

Serves 3–4

NUTRIENT ANALYSIS PER SERVING 1119 kJ – 266 kcal – 44 g protein – 1 g carbohydrate – 1 g sugars – 9 g fat – 3 g saturates – 0 g fibre – 218 mg sodium

HEALTHY TIP Beef and veal in particular are an excellent source of certain B complex vitamins such as vitamin B12. They also contain niacin, zinc, potassium and high-grade protein.

Pork pozole casserole with red sauce

This colourful casserole, known as *pozole*, is made with large maize kernels (hominy) and meat – usually pork – with its broth flavoured with dried chillies. It is traditionally served with a selection of garnishes on the side, which diners add to their dish as they please. Most regions of Mexico have their own *pozole* recipe and their inhabitants fiercely defend their version as being the best. Hominy can be purchased from specialist Mexican food shops or suppliers (by mail order or online).

INGREDIENTS *250 g (8 oz) hominy (pozole corn kernels)* ‖ *500 g (1 lb) boneless leg of pork, cut into bite-sized pieces* ‖ *½ onion* ‖ *1–2 garlic cloves, peeled but kept whole* ‖ *1 celery stick* ‖ *1 bay leaf* ‖ *5 black peppercorns* ‖ *20 g (¾ oz) ancho chillies* ‖ *20 g (¾ oz) guajillo chillies* ‖ *salt*

TO GARNISH *1 heart of cos lettuce, finely sliced* ‖ *1 onion, finely chopped* ‖ *4 limes, cut into wedges* ‖ *8 small radishes, finely sliced* ‖ *8 Tostadas (see page 34)* ‖ *dried oregano* ‖ *chilli powder*

ONE Rinse the hominy and put in a large saucepan with enough water to cover. Bring to the boil, then reduce the heat, cover and simmer for 1½–2 hours until cooked – the kernels must be soft. **TWO** Meanwhile, put the pork in a separate saucepan, cover with water and bring to the boil, skimming the scum that rises to the surface. Add the onion, garlic cloves, celery, bay leaf and peppercorns. Reduce the heat, cover and simmer for 1–1 hour 40 minutes until the meat is cooked and very tender. Remove the meat from the broth, strain the broth and reserve. **THREE** Remove the stems from the chillies, tear the chillies open and remove the seeds (for a milder sauce, remove all the stringy, light-coloured veins as well). Heat a heavy-based frying pan over a medium heat and lightly roast the chillies for a few seconds on both sides. Transfer to a heatproof bowl, cover with boiling water and leave to soak for 15–20 minutes until soft. **FOUR** Drain the chillies, put in a blender or food processor with a little of the soaking water and process to a fairly smooth texture. Pass through a sieve. **FIVE** When the hominy is cooked, add the meat and its broth and bring to the boil. Season to taste with salt and add the chilli sauce. Reduce the heat and simmer for 20 minutes. Check the seasoning. **SIX** Serve very hot in warm individual soup bowls with the garnishes on the side, arranged in separate dishes.

Serves 4

NUTRIENT ANALYSIS PER SERVING (using small tortillas or cut rounds approximately 17 g (½ oz) each) 1640 kJ – 390 kcal – 33 g protein – 36 g carbohydrate – 3 g sugars – 13 g fat – 3 g saturates – 4 g fibre – 210 mg sodium

HEALTHY TIP Select the leaner cuts of meat and trim off the excess fat before cooking, to make this low-fat dish even healthier. If possible, use organic pork.

Pork fillet in pumpkin seed sauce

Pumpkin seed sauce, known as *pipián*, is a pre-Hispanic sauce, and used to be served with fish or game before the arrival of the Spanish, who introduced pork to the country. This delicious and delicate sauce is prepared with *pepitas* – pumpkin seeds – which are a highly nutritious and a very popular ingredient in Mexican cooking.

INGREDIENTS *750 g (1½ lb) pork fillet* ‖ *salt* ‖ *plain White Rice (see page 41 – omit the Poblano Chilli Strips), to serve*

PUMPKIN SEED SAUCE *450 g (14½ oz) tomatillos, husks removed* ‖ *5 green chillies* ‖ *2 garlic cloves, unpeeled* ‖ *25 g (1 oz) fresh coriander* ‖ *1 litre (1¾ pints) chicken stock* ‖ *2 tablespoons vegetable oil* ‖ *250 g (8 oz) pumpkin seeds, shelled and toasted, plus extra to garnish* ‖ *salt*

ONE Lightly sprinkle the pork fillet with salt. Place in a roasting tin and roast in a preheated oven, 220°C (425°F), Gas Mark 7, for 20 minutes. Reduce the oven temperature to 180°C (350°F), Gas Mark 4, and roast for a further 30 minutes or until thoroughly cooked. **TWO** Meanwhile, to make the sauce, heat a dry heavy-based frying pan over a medium heat and roast the tomatillos, chillies and garlic cloves, turning occasionally, until soft. Leave to cool, then peel the garlic. **THREE** Transfer the tomatillos, chillies and garlic to a blender or food processor, add the coriander and half the stock and blend to a fairly smooth texture. Pass through a sieve. **FOUR** Heat the oil in a heavy-based saucepan over a medium heat and gently simmer the sauce for about 10 minutes until cooked. Season to taste with salt. **FIVE** Transfer the mixture again to a blender or food processor, add the pumpkin seeds and the remaining stock and blend to a fairly smooth texture. Check the seasoning. Place in a heatproof dish and keep warm in a large saucepan half-filled with water over a low heat. **SIX** When the meat is ready, transfer the fillet to a warm serving dish, cover loosely with foil and leave to rest for 10 minutes before carving. Slice the pork and serve with the pumpkin seed sauce and the plain White Rice (see page 41), sprinkled with pumpkin seeds to garnish.

Serves 4

NUTRIENT ANALYSIS PER SERVING 2944 kJ – 707 kcal – 56 g protein – 13 g carbohydrate – 4 g sugars – 48 g fat – 10 g saturates – 1 g fibre – 370 mg sodium

HEALTHY TIP Pork tenderloin is an excellent source of protein and thiamine (vitamin B1), essential for energy production, nerve function and muscle tone. The pumpkin seeds are a very good source of several nutrients including manganese, magnesium and phosphorus, as well as protein and monounsaturated fats.

Beef fillet with mushrooms

The cattle farms in the north of the country – where large areas of grassland abound – are famous for the production of high-quality beef. This dish of tender beef fillet with mushrooms is an elegant combination usually served on special occasions.

INGREDIENTS *1 kg (2 lb) beef fillet* ‖ *1 teaspoon olive oil* ‖ *salt and freshly ground pepper*

SAUTÉED MUSHROOMS *2 tablespoons olive oil* ‖ *½ onion, finely chopped* ‖ *3 garlic cloves, finely chopped* ‖ *2–3 red arbol chillies, cut into fine rings* ‖ *750 g (1½ lb) closed cup mushrooms, sliced* ‖ *1 tablespoon finely chopped flat leaf parsley* ‖ *salt and freshly ground black pepper*

ONE Rub the fillet with the oil and lightly sprinkle with salt and pepper. Place in a roasting tin and roast in a preheated oven, 220°C (425°F), Gas Mark 7, for 20 minutes. Reduce the oven temperature to 180°C (350°F), Gas Mark 4, and roast for a further 20 minutes. **TWO** Meanwhile, to make the sautéed mushrooms, heat the oil in a heavy-based saucepan and sauté the onion until translucent. Add the garlic and chillies and sauté for a further minute. Add the mushrooms and sauté for 5–7 minutes until just cooked. Season to taste with salt and pepper and sprinkle the chopped parsley on top. **THREE** When the meat is ready, transfer the fillet to a warm serving dish and leave to rest for 10 minutes before carving. Slice the roast beef and serve with the sautéed mushrooms.

Serves 4

NUTRIENT ANALYSIS PER SERVING 1657 kJ – 395 kcal – 55 g protein – 2 g carbohydrate – 1 g sugars – 19 g fat – 6 g saturates – 5 g fibre – 164 mg sodium

HEALTHY TIP Beef fillet is a very lean cut of meat and an outstanding source of protein. In addition, mushrooms are high in potassium and riboflavin, and also contain phosphorous, copper and iron. Select mushrooms that are firm.

Bricklayer-style fillet

Bricklayer-style is a literal translation of *al albañil*. This term is given to very hot, easy-to-prepare sauces made from a variety of ingredients and eaten by the workers in the construction industry in Mexico City and some other surrounding areas, during the lunch break.

INGREDIENTS *2 tablespoons olive oil* ‖ *750 g (1½ lb) veal fillet, cut into 2.5 cm (1 inch) cubes* ‖ *1 onion, finely sliced lengthways* ‖ *2 garlic cloves, finely sliced lengthways* ‖ *6 hot green chillies, such as jalapeño or serrano, cut into strips (deseeded for a milder taste)* ‖ *2 large ripe tomatoes, skinned, deseeded and finely chopped* ‖ *salt and freshly ground black pepper* ‖ *warm soft corn tortillas, to serve*

ONE Heat 1 tablespoon of the oil in a wok or large heavy-based frying pan over a high heat. Season the meat with salt and pepper and stir-fry in batches until browned. Reserve in a bowl. **TWO** Heat the remaining oil in the pan and stir-fry the onion until translucent. Add the garlic and chillies and sauté for a further minute. **THREE** Return the meat to the pan. Add the tomatoes, season to taste with salt and pepper and stir-fry for a few more minutes until cooked. **FOUR** Serve immediately with warm corn tortillas.

Serves 4

NUTRIENT ANALYSIS PER SERVING 1170 kJ – 279 kcal – 40 g protein – 5 g carbohydrate – 4 g sugars – 11 g fat – 3 g saturates – 1 g fibre – 216 mg sodium

HEALTHY TIP Besides being the best source of protein, meat, especially red meat, contains iron, which is essential for the formation of red blood cells and the functioning of the nervous system. In addition, the chillies and vegetables increase the vitamin and mineral content of this dish.

Leg of lamb with adobo sauce

Adobo is a sauce made from puréed dried chillies, herbs and vinegar as the main ingredients. It is used as a serving sauce as well as a marinade for meats. This aromatic sauce complements the flavour of the lamb perfectly in this recipe.

INGREDIENTS *1 x 1.5–2 kg (3–4 lb) leg of lamb* ‖ *1 tablespoon olive oil* ‖ *2 garlic cloves, crushed* ‖ *salt and freshly ground black pepper* ‖ *wild rocket leaves, to garnish (optional)*
ADOBO SAUCE *4–5 ancho chillies, deseeded* ‖ *1 small onion* ‖ *4 garlic cloves* ‖ *1 teaspoon dried oregano* ‖ *½ teaspoon dried thyme* ‖ *2 tablespoons cider vinegar* ‖ *300 ml (½ pint) chicken stock* ‖ *1 tablespoon vegetable oil*

ONE Rub the lamb with the oil and garlic, season with salt and pepper and place in a roasting tin. Roast in a preheated oven, 220°C (425°F), Gas Mark 7, for 20 minutes. Reduce the oven temperature to 180°C (350°F), Gas Mark 4, and roast for a further 50 minutes per kg (2 lb), basting occasionally. The meat should still be pink inside. **TWO** Meanwhile, to make the sauce, remove the stems from the chillies, tear the chillies open and remove the seeds. Heat a dry, heavy-based frying pan over a medium heat and lightly roast the chillies for a few seconds on both sides. Transfer to a heatproof bowl, cover with boiling water and leave to soak for 15–20 minutes until soft. **THREE** Drain the chillies and transfer to a blender or food processor. Add the remaining ingredients, except the oil, and process until smooth. Pass through a sieve. **FOUR** Heat the oil in a saucepan over a medium heat, add the chilli mixture and simmer gently, stirring constantly, for about 15 minutes until cooked. If the sauce gets too thick, add a little more stock. Keep warm. **FIVE** When the meat is ready, transfer to a warm plate and cover loosely with foil. Leave to rest for 10 minutes before carving. Slice the meat and serve covered with the adobo sauce, garnished with rocket leaves if liked.

Serves 4

NUTRIENT ANALYSIS PER SERVING 1485 kJ – 360 kcal – 57 g protein – 3 g carbohydrate – 2 g sugars – 34 g fat – 13 g saturates – 0 g fibre – 1344 mg sodium

HEALTHY TIP Lamb is a good source of protein and essential vitamins and minerals, such as zinc, which is highly valuable for its beneficial effects on the immune system.

Beef salpicón

A *salpicón* is a combination of different ingredients including shredded meat or fish. In the Yucatan Peninsula, in the south of the country, it is prepared in the old-fashioned way using shredded venison. Since deer is a protected species, beef is now more commonly used to prepare this traditional dish.

INGREDIENTS *500 g (1 lb) beef skirt, cut into large squares* ‖ *½ onion, kept whole, and ½ onion, finely chopped* ‖ *1 garlic clove, peeled* ‖ *1 celery stick* ‖ *1 bay leaf* ‖ *2 tablespoons finely chopped fresh coriander* ‖ *6–8 cos lettuce leaves, finely shredded* ‖ *1 large ripe avocado, peeled, stoned and diced* ‖ *1 large tomato, diced* ‖ *2 chipotle chillies, bottled or canned in adobo sauce, deseeded and finely sliced, or 2–3 green chillies, deseeded and cut into thin strips* ‖ *6 radishes, finely sliced* ‖ *75 g (3 oz) feta cheese, crumbled* ‖ *salt and freshly ground black pepper*

DRESSING *150 ml (¼ pint) extra virgin olive oil* ‖ *50 ml (2 fl oz) cider vinegar* ‖ *½ teaspoon dried oregano* ‖ *salt and freshly ground black pepper*

ONE Put the meat in a saucepan and cover with water. Bring to the boil, skimming the scum that rises to the surface. Add the whole onion half, garlic clove, celery, bay leaf, salt and pepper to taste. Cover and simmer for 1½–2 hours until the meat is very tender. Leave to cool slightly in the broth. **TWO** Remove the meat from the broth and shred into fine strands (reserve the broth for some other use). Add the chopped onion and coriander. Mix all the dressing ingredients together and pour two-thirds over the meat. Mix well, cover and leave to stand for 20 minutes. **THREE** Just before serving, make a bed of shredded lettuce in a serving dish. Place the meat mixture on the lettuce. Garnish with pieces of avocado alternating with the tomato and chipotle slices or green chilli strips. Drizzle the remaining dressing over the salad. Scatter over the radish slices and the feta, and serve immediately.

Serves 4

NUTRIENT ANALYSIS PER SERVING 3060 kJ – 740 kcal – 30 g protein – 4 g carbohydrate – 3 g sugars – 67 g fat – 19 g saturates – 1 g fibre – 350 mg sodium

HEALTHY TIP Combining the meat with vegetables provides both high-quality protein from the meat and dietary fibre and other nutrients from the vegetables.

Beef and vegetable casserole with dried chilli sauce

This is one of the most delicious and healthy stews in Mexican cuisine. Meat and vegetables are gently cooked and seasoned with dried chillies. Traditionally, small balls made with masa harina – *chochoyotes* – are cooked in the broth.

INGREDIENTS *625 g (1¼ lb) beef skirt or topside, diced* ‖ *1 onion* ‖ *2 garlic cloves, 1 peeled* ‖ *1 celery stick* ‖ *1 bay leaf* ‖ *5 black peppercorns* ‖ *2 corn-on-the-cob, cut into chunks* ‖ *2 courgettes, halved and cut lengthways into quarters* ‖ *1 carrot, halved and cut lengthways into quarters* ‖ *5 pasilla chillies* ‖ *1 teaspoon vegetable oil* ‖ *2 fresh epazote sprigs (if available)* ‖ *65 g (2½ oz) masa harina* ‖ *salt* ‖ *warm soft corn tortillas, to serve*

ONE Put the meat in a saucepan and cover with water. Bring to the boil, skimming the scum that rises to the surface. Add half the onion, the peeled garlic clove, celery, bay leaf and peppercorns. Cover and simmer for 1½–2 hours until the meat is tender. Remove the meat from the broth, strain the broth and reserve. **TWO** Cook the corn, courgettes and carrot separately in boiling water until just tender. Strain and reserve the vegetables and cooking water. **THREE** Remove the stems from the chillies, tear the chillies open and remove the seeds. Heat a dry heavy-based frying pan over a medium heat and lightly roast the chillies for a few seconds on both sides. Soak the chillies in boiling water for 15–20 minutes until soft. **FOUR** Meanwhile, place the unpeeled garlic and the remaining onion, halved, in the frying pan and roast, turning occasionally, until soft. Leave to cool, then peel the garlic. **FIVE** Drain the chillies and transfer to a blender or food processor with some of the soaking water. Add the garlic and onion and blend until smooth, then sieve. **SIX** Heat the oil in a saucepan, add the chilli mixture and simmer for about 15 minutes. Add the meat broth, epazote and salt to taste. **SEVEN** Mix the masa harina with about 75 ml (3 fl oz) water and knead to a soft dough. Mould into 1 cm (½ inch) balls and press your finger into the centre of each. Add to the casserole and gently simmer for 15 minutes. **EIGHT** Add the meat and vegetables, with some of the reserved vegetable cooking water, if needed. Check the seasoning and simmer for a further 10 minutes. Serve very hot in warmed individual soup plates with warm corn tortillas.

Serves 4

NUTRIENT ANALYSIS PER SERVING 1687 kJ – 403 kcal – 35 g protein – 22 g carbohydrate – 4 g sugars – 20 g fat – 7 g saturates – 2 g fibre – 323 mg sodium

HEALTHY TIP Beef is an excellent source of protein, potassium, zinc and certain B complex vitamins. The vegetables are low in fat, contain no cholesterol and provide soluble and insoluble fibre.

Vegetables and salads

Watercress, grapefruit and avocado salad

Watercress is extensively cultivated in the centre of the country and is usually eaten raw in salads, as in this colourful dish, whose ingredients offer an elegant combination of flavours and textures.

INGREDIENTS *2 red or pink grapefruit* ‖ *2 large ripe avocados* ‖ *65 g (2½ oz) watercress, washed* ‖ *8–10 small radishes, finely sliced* ‖ *4 spring onions, cut diagonally into thin slices*
VINAIGRETTE *6 tablespoons olive oil* ‖ *2 tablespoons cider vinegar* ‖ *½ teaspoon clear honey* ‖ *½ teaspoon Dijon mustard* ‖ *salt and freshly ground black pepper*

ONE Peel the grapefruit. Divide into segments and remove the membranes and seeds. **TWO** Mix all the vinaigrette ingredients together thoroughly. **THREE** Just before serving, half the avocados and remove the stones. Peel and slice the flesh. Place in a bowl with the remaining salad ingredients. Add the dressing and toss gently. Check the seasoning. **FOUR** Serve in individual salad dishes.

Serves 4

NUTRIENT ANALYSIS PER SERVING 1233 kJ – 297 kcal – 3 g protein – 13 g carbohydrate – 12 g sugars – 27 g fat – 4 g saturates – 3 g fibre – 40 mg sodium

HEALTHY TIP Watercress is a powerful detoxifier, rich in vitamins and minerals, especially vitamins A and C, zinc and iron. Grapefruit is an excellent source of vitamin C, which helps to support the immune system. The avocados are a good source of potassium and dietary fibre. They also help towards maintaing a healthy blood pressure.

Tomato salad

Tomatoes are a very important ingredient in Mexican cuisine. Their use has no limits – cooked, roasted, grilled or raw, for salsas, soups, moles or casseroles, all Mexicans love tomatoes. This simple and flavourful salad makes a healthy accompaniment for plain cooked fish, meat or poultry. It is on the menu of most restaurants and cafés in Mexico.

INGREDIENTS *4 large ripe tomatoes* ‖ *1 onion, sliced* ‖ *dried oregano, to taste*

DRESSING *6 tablespoons extra virgin olive oil* ‖ *2 tablespoons cider vinegar* ‖ *1 garlic clove, crushed* ‖ *½ teaspoon Dijon mustard* ‖ *salt and freshly ground black pepper*

ONE Slice the tomatoes and arrange them on a platter. **TWO** Slice the onion and submerge in iced water for at least 10 minutes (to tame the sharpness of the onion). Drain, rinse and pat dry. Place on top of the tomatoes. **THREE** Mix all the dressing ingredients together thoroughly, drizzle over the tomatoes and onion and sprinkle the oregano on top. Serve at room temperature.

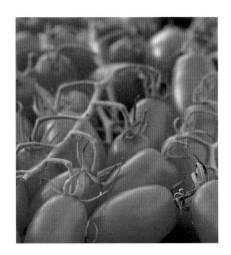

Serves 4

NUTRIENT ANALYSIS PER SERVING 753 kJ – 182 kcal – 1 g protein – 6 g carbohydrate – 6 g sugars – 17 g fat – 3 g saturates – 2 g fibre – 38 mg sodium

HEALTHY TIP Tomatoes are rich in vitamins A and C, also contain vitamin B and are a good source of calcium, phosphorus, potassium, sodium and dietary fibre. Onions contain a fair amount of vitamin C with traces of other vitamins and minerals well known for their health benefits.

Apple and walnut salad

Chihuahua, a state in northern Mexico, produces a large quantity of apples, which are used in many dishes. Apples are eaten fresh all over the country and it is a tradition to prepare apple salad at Christmas time. This salad is an ideal accompaniment for turkey.

INGREDIENTS *2 dessert apples, such as Golden Delicious* ‖ *3 fresh pineapple slices* ‖ *50 g (2 oz) walnuts* ‖ *2 celery sticks, finely sliced* ‖ *2 tablespoons mayonnaise* ‖ *salt and freshly ground black pepper*

ONE Peel, core and dice the apples. Dice the pineapple. Roughly chop the walnuts. **TWO** Mix the fruit and walnuts with the celery. Fold the mayonnaise thoroughly into the fruit and nut mixture and season to taste with salt and pepper. **THREE** Serve at room temperature.

Serves 4

NUTRIENT ANALYSIS PER SERVING 830 kJ – 199 kcal – 3 g protein – 16 g carbohydrate – 16 g sugars – 15 g fat – 2 g saturates – 3 g fibre – 47 mg sodium

HEALTHY TIP Highly nutritious and cleansing, apples are a good source of fibre and vitamins A and C. They are also rich in the powerful flavonoid quercetin, which acts as an antioxidant and may prevent some cancers and protect the arteries and heart. Walnuts are a good source of protein, iron and calcium.

Green bean and new potato salad

Cooked fresh vegetables are frequently prepared as side dishes throughout the country. This colourful and healthy salad is usually served to accompany fish, meat or poultry dishes, especially during summertime.

INGREDIENTS *200 g (7 oz) green beans* ‖ *200 g (7 oz) baby new potatoes, cooked in their skins* ‖ *½ red onion, finely sliced, lengthways* ‖ *½ teaspoon dried oregano*

DRESSING *1 tablespoon cider vinegar* ‖ *3 tablespoons extra virgin olive oil* ‖ *1 small garlic clove, finely chopped* ‖ *¼ teaspoon caster sugar* ‖ *salt and freshly ground black pepper*

ONE Trim the tops of the green beans, leaving the tails on. Blanch the beans in a saucepan of boiling salted water for 1 minute. Drain and place on a tray to cool rapidly. **TWO** Slice the cooked potatoes diagonally and place them in a large salad bowl. Mix in the red onion and green beans. **THREE** Mix all the dressing ingredients together throroughly, drizzle over the vegetables and toss gently. Arrange the salad on a platter, sprinkle with the oregano and serve immediately.

Serves 4

NUTRIENT ANALYSIS PER SERVING 549 kJ – 132 kcal – 2 g protein – 12 g carbohydrate – 4 g sugars – 9 g fat – 1 g saturates – 2 g fibre – 7 mg sodium

HEALTHY TIP While relatively low in calories, this salad is loaded with nutrients. Both green beans and potatoes are very good sources of vitamin C, manganese, potassium, calcium and dietary fibre.

Grilled courgettes with goats' cheese

Courgettes are a favourite vegetable in Mexico and are used in many regional dishes. A popular choice is the combination of courgettes with fresh white cheese.

INGREDIENTS *5 large courgettes, diagonally sliced* ‖ *1 tablespoon olive oil* ‖ *salt and freshly ground black pepper* ‖ *1 tablespoon extra virgin olive oil* ‖ *1–2 garlic cloves, finely diced* ‖ *100 g (3½ oz) soft goats' cheese* ‖ *30 g (1 oz) pine nuts, toasted*

ONE Brush the courgette slices with olive oil and cook in a hot griddle pan for 1–2 minutes each side. The courgettes should be cooked, but still firm. Season to taste with salt and pepper. Heat the extra virgin olive oil in a small frying pan over a medium heat and gently sauté the garlic for 1 minute. **TWO** Transfer the courgettes to a warm serving plate. Crumble the goats' cheese over the courgettes, scatter over the pine nuts and drizzle the garlic oil on top. Serve immediately.

Serves 4

NUTRIENT ANALYSIS PER SERVING 710 kJ – 170 kcal – 6 g protein – 3 g carbohydrate – 3 g sugars – 15 g fat – 4 g saturates – 1 g fibre – 125 mg sodium

HEALTHY TIP Courgettes are low in calories and a good source of beta-carotene, which the body converts into vitamin A. They also are a useful source of vitamin C and folate. Pine nuts, being high in protein and essential fat, are a good meat substitute for vegetarians.

Nopalitos salad

This colourful salad is a traditional way to prepare *nopales* (cactus leaves), called *nopalitos* when cut into small pieces. It is very popular all over Mexico but mainly consumed in the central states of the country, where you can see this delicious salad displayed in attractive large earthenware containers, ready to be sold at local markets. Nopales can be obtained from specialist Mexican food shops or suppliers.

INGREDIENTS *350 g (11½ oz) nopales, fresh, bottled or canned* ‖ *1 small onion, finely chopped* ‖ *2–3 serrano or jalapeño chillies, sliced (deseeded for a milder taste)* ‖ *4 tablespoons chopped fresh coriander*
DRESSING *3 tablespoons extra virgin olive oil* ‖ *1 tablespoon cider vinegar* ‖ *½ teaspoon dried oregano* ‖ *salt*
TO GARNISH *2 large ripe tomatoes, skinned, deseeded and sliced or finely chopped* ‖ *4 spring onions, white and green parts, diagonally sliced* ‖ *150 g (5 oz) feta cheese, crumbled*

ONE If you are using fresh nopales, cut them into 1 cm (½ inch) squares and cook in a large saucepan of boiling water for about 20 minutes until tender. Drain and leave to cool. If using bottled or canned nopales, drain, rinse thoroughly and pat dry. Cut into small squares. **TWO** Mix the nopales, onion, chillies and coriander together in a bowl. **THREE** Mix all the dressing ingredients together thoroughly and pour over the nopalitos salad. Mix gently until all the vegetables are coated. Check the seasoning. **FOUR** Arrange the nopalitos salad on a serving dish. Place the tomatoes on top and scatter with the spring onions and feta. Serve at room temperature.

Serves 4

NUTRIENT ANALYSIS PER SERVING 858 kJ – 207 kcal – 8 g protein – 8 g carbohydrate – 6 g sugars – 16 g fat – 6 g saturates – 3 g fibre – 570 mg sodium
HEALTHY TIP Nopales have many nutritional and medicinal properties. One of their greatest assets is the large amount of dietary fibre they contain. They are a good source of vitamin A, vitamin C and calcium.

Baby new potatoes in tomatillo sauce

This dish is an excellent accompaniment for steamed or grilled fish or meat such as pork and chicken. It is very popular in informal eateries for workers in the big cities and can be eaten as a main meal with beans and warm corn tortillas.

INGREDIENTS *500 g (1 lb) tomatillos, husks removed* ‖ *2 green chillies, deseeded* ‖ *6 tablespoons roughly chopped fresh coriander, plus extra to garnish* ‖ *1 tablespoon vegetable oil* ‖ *1 onion, finely chopped* ‖ *500 g (1 lb) baby new potatoes, parboiled in their skins* ‖ *salt*

ONE Put the tomatillos, chillies and coriander in a blender or food processor and blend until smooth. **TWO** Heat the oil in a heavy-based frying pan over a medium heat and sauté the onion until soft. Add the tomatillo mixture and season to taste with salt. Cook for about 10 minutes. **THREE** Add the potatoes to the sauce and gently simmer for 5 minutes until fully cooked. **FOUR** Transfer to a serving dish and serve, garnished with coriander.

Serves 4

NUTRIENT ANALYSIS PER SERVING 586 kJ – 138 kcal – 3 g protein – 25 g carbohydrate – 6 g sugars – 4 g fat – 1 g saturates – 3 g fibre – 26 mg sodium

HEALTHY TIP Tomatillos are rich in vitamin A and also offer a good amount of vitamin C, as do the potatoes, which are also a very good source of vegetable protein and dietary fibre.

Pickled vegetables

Pickles are a classic feature of Mexican cuisine. Pickled chillies, especially the jalapeño variety, are a favourite and are usually combined with carrots and onions. Nowadays, a wider selection of pickled vegetables are offered as a starter or side dish. Along the coast of Mexico, fish and shellfish pickled dishes are very popular.

INGREDIENTS *3 tablespoons olive oil* ‖ *16 spring onions, white parts only* ‖ *4 carrots, cut into sticks* ‖ *4 garlic cloves, peeled* ‖ *2 green chillies, preferably jalapeño* ‖ *150 g (5 oz) cauliflower florets* ‖ *16 small yellow- or red-skinned potatoes, cooked in their skins* ‖ *150 g (5 oz) button mushrooms* ‖ *350 ml (12 fl oz) cider vinegar* ‖ *175 ml (6 fl oz) water* ‖ *½ teaspoon dried thyme* ‖ *½ teaspoon dried oregano* ‖ *2 bay leaves* ‖ *1 teaspoon salt* ‖ *freshly ground black pepper*

ONE Heat the oil in a large heavy-based frying pan and sauté the spring onions, carrots and garlic cloves over a medium heat for 2 minutes. Add the chillies (halve to obtain a strong chilli flavour) and cauliflower and sauté for 2 minutes. Add the potatoes and mushrooms and sauté for a further minute. **TWO** Put the vinegar, measured water, herbs, salt and pepper to taste in a saucepan and bring to the boil. Pour over the vegetables, then immediately remove from the heat. Leave to cool completely. **THREE** Pour into a glass container, cover and refrigerate for at least 1 day before using. **FOUR** To keep long-term, pack into sterilized jars, seal and store in a cool, dark place for up to 1 year.

Serves 4

NUTRIENT ANALYSIS PER SERVING 880 kJ – 210 kcal – 6 g protein – 27 g carbohydrate – 11 g sugars – 10 g fat – 2 g saturates – 5 g fibre – 545 mg sodium

HEALTHY TIP In general, vegetables provide a range of vitamins and minerals, particularly A, B6, C and folic acid. They also provide potassium, iron, magnesium and calcium, and are low in fat and contain no cholesterol. Choose the best quality fresh vegetables, organic if possible.

Baby spinach and mushroom salad

This elegant and refreshing salad is the perfect choice for a healthy meal. It makes a particularly delicious accompaniment to simple healthy dishes such as grilled fish, roasted meat and poultry or a plain omelette.

INGREDIENTS *2 teaspoons sesame seeds* ‖ *125 g (4 oz) baby spinach* ‖ *175 g (6 oz) white cup mushrooms* ‖ *3 tablespoons vegetable oil* ‖ *salt and freshly ground black pepper*

ONE Heat a dry non-stick frying pan over a medium heat and toast the sesame seeds for a few seconds to enhance their nutty flavour. **TWO** Thoroughly wash and dry the spinach. Wipe the mushrooms with damp kitchen paper, trim the tips of the stalks and thinly slice. **THREE** Arrange the spinach and mushrooms on a salad plate and drizzle with the oil. Season to taste with salt and pepper. Scatter the toasted sesame seeds on top of the salad and serve immediately.

Serves 4

NUTRIENT ANALYSIS PER SERVING 410 kJ – 100 kcal – 2 g protein – 1 g carbohydrate – 1 g sugars – 10 g fat – 1 g saturates – 2 g fibre – 46 mg sodium

HEALTHY TIP This salad offers an excellent source of important vitamins and minerals. Sesame seeds contain powerful antioxidants that are anti-carcinogenic. Raw spinach is an excellent source of folic acid.

Potato patties

Potato patties are prepared all over the country. In central Mexico, especially during Lent, this could be the main dish of a family meal at lunchtime and is traditionally served with lettuce and salsa mexicana.

INGREDIENTS *500 g (1 lb) potatoes, unpeeled* ‖ *100 g (3½ oz) feta cheese, crumbled* ‖ *20 g (¾ oz) unsalted butter* ‖ *1 organic free-range egg yolk* ‖ *plain flour, for flouring* ‖ *vegetable oil, for oiling* ‖ *salt and freshly ground black pepper*

TO SERVE *lettuce leaves, torn into bite-sized pieces (optional)* ‖ *lemon wedges (optional)* ‖ *Salsa Mexicana (see page 90)*

ONE Cook the potatoes whole in their skins in boiling water until tender. Drain and leave to cool slightly. When cool enough to handle, peel, then mash the potatoes while still warm. **TWO** Place the mashed potatoes in a bowl, add the feta, butter and egg yolk and stir until well mixed. Season to taste with salt and pepper. **THREE** Divide the mixture into 9 equal portions and, with floured hands, shape into flattish circles about 7 cm (3 inches) in diameter. Place on a lightly oiled baking sheet and bake in a preheated oven, 180°C (350°F), Gas Mark 4, for about 15 minutes, then turn over and bake for a further 10 minutes until golden brown. **FOUR** Serve warm with lettuce and lemon wedges, if using, and Salsa Mexicana (see page 90).

Serves 3–4

NUTRIENT ANALYSIS PER SERVING 1394 kJ – 334 kcal – 10 g protein – 34 g carbohydrate – 2 g sugars – 18 g fat – 9 g saturates – 3 g fibre – 500 mg sodium

HEALTHY TIP Baking the potato cakes in the oven rather than frying them, the traditional cooking method, makes these patties even healthier. Potatoes are very good source of vegetable protein, potassium, vitamin C, iron, phosphorous, niacin, enzymes and dietary fibre.

Crème caramel

One of Mexico's favourite desserts, the origins of crème caramel can be traced back to the Spanish Conquest, like so many of the country's puddings, when milk and eggs were introduced. Egg custard is popular in many cuisines all around the country, but the signature of this dish is its caramelized sugar topping.

INGREDIENTS *150 g (5 oz) granulated sugar* ‖ *3 organic free-range eggs* ‖ *1 organic free-range egg yolk* ‖ *300 ml (½ pint) semi-skimmed milk* ‖ *400 g (13 oz) canned condensed milk* ‖ *1 teaspoon vanilla extract*

ONE Warm a soufflé or other ovenproof dish in a preheated oven, 160°C (325°F), Gas Mark 3. **TWO** Put the sugar in a heavy-based saucepan over a low heat and allow it to melt slowly. When melted, boil rapidly until it has turned to a brown caramel. Pour into the hot soufflé or other dish and coat all over by carefully tipping the dish. Leave to cool. **THREE** Beat the eggs and egg yolk in a bowl until creamy. Add the milk, condensed milk and vanilla extract and mix well. Pour into the prepared dish. Cover with a piece of foil, but don't let it touch the custard. Stand the dish in a roasting tin half-filled with hot water and cook in the preheated oven for 1 hour or until the custard has set. **FOUR** Remove from the oven and leave to cool. Cover and chill in the refrigerator for at least 2 hours. **FIVE** To serve, run the tip of a pointed knife around the edge of the dish to loosen the custard and invert on to a deep serving dish, allowing the caramel to run over the top and sides.

Serves 6

NUTRIENT ANALYSIS PER SERVING 1665 kJ – 394 kcal – 11 g protein – 66 g carbohydrate – 66 g sugars – 11 g fat – 6 g saturates – 0 g fibre – 160 mg sodium

HEALTHY TIP In order to make the traditional recipe for this custard lighter, the quantity of egg yolks and sugar has been reduced, but it still retains an optimum balance for a great flavour and texture.

Rice pudding

In this popular Spanish dessert, rice is cooked in milk with sugar, cinnamon and raisins. Its consistency can be liquid or thick and it can be served warm, cold or at room temperature. In Mexico City it is usually served cold as a lunchtime dessert at home or in restaurants or cafés, while in other parts of the country it is served warm for breakfast.

INGREDIENTS *200 g (7 oz) long-grain white rice* | *1.5 litres (2½ pints) semi-skimmed milk* | *100 g (3½ oz) caster sugar* | *pinch of salt* | *1 vanilla pod* | *1 cinnamon stick, broken into 2–3 pieces* | *thinly pared rind of 1 lime* | *thinly pared rind of 1 orange* | *50 g (2 oz) raisins* | *ground cinnamon, to decorate*

ONE Rinse the rice briefly to remove any impurities, drain and soak for 15 minutes in boiling water. Rinse well and drain. Put the milk, sugar, salt, vanilla pod, cinnamon stick and lime and orange rind in a heavy-based saucepan. Bring slowly to the boil, stirring constantly. Remove from the heat and leave to infuse for 10 minutes. Remove the lime and orange rind, then remove the vanilla pod, slit open and scrape out the seeds into the milk. **TWO** Add the rice to the milk and bring to the boil over a medium heat. Reduce the heat, cover and gently simmer until the rice is cooked and the mixture thickens. Stir in the raisins. You may need some more cold milk to adjust the consistency – the rice must not be dry. **THREE** Remove from the heat and leave to cool, then transfer the pudding to a serving dish, cover and refrigerate until required. **FOUR** Serve cold, dusted with cinnamon to decorate.

Serves 6–8

NUTRIENT ANALYSIS PER SERVING 1376 kJ – 324 kcal – 11 g protein – 65 g carbohydrate – 36 g sugars – 4 g fat – 3 g saturates – 1 g fibre – 145 mg sodium

HEALTHY TIP Rice, which is cholesterol- and gluten-free, is low in sodium, contains only a trace of fat and is an excellent source of complex carbohydrates. Semi-skimmed milk is a good source of calcium and contains only 2 per cent fat.

Quince paste

Because of its high pectin content, quince is particularly good in jams, jellies and preserves. Quince paste is of Arab origin and was introduced to Mexico by the Spanish. It is usually served with Manchego cheese or panela, a fresh white Mexican cheese.

INGREDIENTS *1 kg (2 lb) quinces* ‖ *granulated sugar* ‖ *250 ml (8 fl oz) water* ‖ *Manchego cheese, to serve*

ONE Wash and quarter the quinces. Place in a saucepan, cover with water and bring to the boil. Reduce the heat and simmer for 30–45 minutes until soft. Drain and leave to cool slightly. When cool enough to handle, peel and core, then transfer to a blender or food processor and purée while still warm. Weigh the quince purée. **TWO** Place a quantity of granulated sugar equal in weight to the weight of the quince purée in a heavy-based saucepan, add the measured water and heat slowly, stirring constantly, until the sugar has completely dissolved. **THREE** Increase the heat, bring to the boil and boil until the syrup reaches soft ball point (115°C/239°F, or when a drop will form a soft ball when dropped in cold water). Add the quince purée to the sugar syrup and cook, stirring constantly, for about 30 minutes until thick and the paste leaves the sides of the pan. **FOUR** Transfer the paste to a loaf tin lined with greaseproof paper and leave in an airing cupboard for 3–4 days. Turn out on to a plate and leave to dry completely. You can then store the paste for up to 1 year in an airtight container. **FIVE** Slice and serve at room temperature with slices or shavings of Manchego cheese.

Makes 18 slices

NUTRIENT ANALYSIS PER SERVING 620 kJ – 146 kcal – 0 g protein – 39 g carbohydrate – 39 g sugars – 0 g fat – 0 g saturates – 3 g fibre – 0 mg sodium

HEALTHY TIP Quinces are an excellent source of vitamin C, a powerful booster of the immune system and well known for their ability to increase resistance to infections and disease. They also contain fibre and riboflavin.

Roasted wild berries

A great variety of fruits grow in Mexico all year round and often seasonal fruits are the only item offered as dessert after a meal. In this recipe, the berries are lightly roasted to release their natural sweetness, resulting in an elegant and delicious dessert.

INGREDIENTS *150 g (5 oz) small fresh strawberries* ‖ *125 g (4 oz) fresh blueberries* ‖ *125 g (4 oz) fresh raspberries* ‖ *125 g (4 oz) fresh blackberries* ‖ *1 tablespoon caster sugar (optional)* ‖ *mint sprigs, to decorate (optional)*

ONE Rinse and hull the strawberries and rinse the blueberries, then drain well and place on kitchen paper to dry. Gently wipe the raspberries and blackberries. **TWO** Gently warm the strawberries in a heavy-based saucepan over a medium heat, stirring constantly. Add the sugar, if using, then add the blueberries, raspberries and blackberries and cook for about 1 minute; don't let the fruit become soggy. **THREE** Immediately transfer to a serving plate and decorate with mint sprigs, if liked. Serve warm.

Serves 4

NUTRIENT ANALYSIS PER SERVING 212 kJ – 50 kcal – 1 g protein – 11 g carbohydrate – 11 g sugars – 0 g fat – 0 g saturates – 6 g fibre – 0 mg sodium

HEALTHY TIP This mix of berries is an excellent source of vitamins A and C, and rich in calcium, magnesium, potassium, beta-carotene and folic acid.

Sweet potato and pineapple dessert
This classic dessert is traditionally made with *camote*, a tuber very similar to the sweet potato, which was cultivated by the inhabitants of Mesoamerica before the arrival of the Spanish. Nowadays in Mexican homes it is mainly prepared as a purée or soft paste, cooked with sugar and often mixed with fruit, such as guava, coconut or pineapple.

INGREDIENTS *400 g (13 oz) sweet potatoes* ‖ *250 g (8 oz) pineapple slices* ‖ *100 g (3½ oz) sugar* ‖ *1 cinnamon stick*

TO DECORATE *20 g (¾ oz) raisins* ‖ *20 g (¾ oz) flaked almonds, toasted*

ONE Wash the sweet potatoes, place in a large saucepan and cover with water. Bring to the boil, then reduce the heat and simmer for 25–30 minutes until cooked. Drain and leave to cool. **TWO** Peel the sweet potatoes, roughly chop and place in a blender or food processor. Add the pineapple and blend until smooth. Pass the mixture through a sieve into a saucepan and add the sugar and the cinnamon stick. Cook over a medium heat, stirring constantly, for about 30 minutes until you can see the base of the pan. Check the sweetness – if the pineapple is not sweet enough, you may need to add a little extra sugar. **THREE** Remove the cinnamon stick, spread the mixture in a serving dish and leave to cool. **FOUR** Decorate with the raisins and toasted almonds, and serve at room temperature.

Serves 4

NUTRIENT ANALYSIS PER SERVING 1087 kJ – 255 kcal – 3 g protein – 58 g carbohydrate – 42 g sugars – 3 g fat – 0 g saturates – 4 g fibre – 45 mg sodium

HEALTHY TIP Sweet potato is an exceptional source of vitamin A and also provides vitamin C, calcium, iron, potassium, phosphorus and sodium.

Walnut jamoncillo

Jamoncillo is the name given to different kinds of firm and soft desserts made with milk slowly cooked with sugar and other ingredients such as almonds, walnuts, pine nuts, pumpkin seeds and strawberries. This sweet delicacy is traditionally sold at popular fairs and religious festivities.

INGREDIENTS *1 large organic free-range egg* ‖ *450 g (14½ oz) walnuts, ground, plus extra, roughly chopped, to decorate* ‖ *175 g (6 oz) granulated sugar* ‖ *250 ml (8 fl oz) semi-skimmed milk*

ONE Beat the egg and place in a heavy-based saucepan with the ground walnuts, sugar and milk. Mix together thoroughly. **TWO** Cook over a medium heat, stirring constantly, for 30–35 minutes until you can see the base of the pan. **THREE** Remove from the heat and continue stirring for a few more minutes until it starts to set. **FOUR** Transfer the walnut mixture to a shallow square dish. Leave to cool completely. **FIVE** When solid, cut into 2.5 cm (1 inch) cubes and top each cube with a piece of walnut. Place in a serving dish and serve.

Makes about 60 cubes

NUTRIENT ANALYSIS PER SERVING 287 kJ – 69 kcal – 1 g protein – 4 g carbohydrate – 4 g sugars – 6 g fat – 1 g saturates – 1 g fibre – 0 mg sodium

HEALTHY TIP Walnuts are an excellent source of omega-3 essential fatty acids, a special type of protective fat that the body cannot manufacture. They also are a good source of protein, iron and calcium.

Fresh fruit jelly

A particular favourite in Mexico, jellies are prepared for special occasions as well as everyday desserts at lunchtime. Fruit jellies contain a generous amount of fresh fruit, the type of fruit used varying according to the season and family traditions.

INGREDIENTS *4 tablespoons water* ‖ *5 teaspoons powdered gelatine* ‖ *600 ml (1 pint) cranberry juice* ‖ *¼ cantaloupe melon, peeled and deseeded (about 125 g/4 oz), diced* ‖ *½ peeled and stoned mango (about 75 g/3 oz), diced* ‖ *1 peeled and cored apple (about 100 g/3½ oz), diced* ‖ *150 g (5 oz) seedless red grapes* ‖ *150 g (5 oz) seedless green grapes* ‖ *125 g (4 oz) fresh strawberries, hulled and quartered*

ONE Put the measured water in a small saucepan. Sprinkle over the gelatine and leave for 5 minutes until spongy. Place over a very low heat to dissolve, without either boiling or stirring, until it becomes liquid and clear. **TWO** Warm 150 ml (¼ pint) of the cranberry juice and mix into the gelatine. Add the remaining cranberry juice and stir well. **THREE** Wet the base of individual bowls or a 20 cm (8 inch) diameter jelly mould and cover with some of the gelatine mixture. Chill in the refrigerator for about 20 minutes until beginning to set. **FOUR** Arrange the fruit over the gelatine, pour three-quarters of the jelly over the fruit and refrigerate for about 20 minutes until beginning to set, then add the remaining jelly. (This is to ensure that the jelly has a flat base when turned out.) Refrigerate for 2–4 hours until completely set. **FIVE** Run the tip of a pointed knife around the edge of the mould to loosen. Place a damp serving plate over the mould and turn both the plate and mould over together. Give a sharp shake and lift the mould. Serve chilled.

Serves 6

NUTRIENT ANALYSIS PER SERVING 456 kJ – 107 kcal – 2 g protein – 25 g carbohydrate – 14 g sugars – 0 g fat – 0 g saturates – 2 g fibre – 9 mg sodium

HEALTHY TIP While each type of fruit has its own specific composition of nutritional elements, fruit in general has certain common characteristics. Most fruits have a high water content and are a good source of vitamin A, vitamin B6, vitamin C, potassium, calcium, iron and magnesium.

Corn cake

Corn cake is baked all over Mexico throughout the whole year, especially of course at harvest time, between July and September. It is usually served for breakfast or dinner with coffee or hot chocolate. It can be sweet or savoury and sometimes it is offered as a side dish with mole sauce or poblano chilli strips, as in central Mexico.

INGREDIENTS *500 g (1 lb) fresh sweetcorn kernels* ‖ *65 g (2½ oz) butter, melted, plus extra for greasing* ‖ *65 g (2½ oz) caster sugar* ‖ *65 g (2½ oz) plain flour* ‖ *3 organic free-range eggs* ‖ *1 tablespoon baking powder* ‖ *¼ teaspoon salt* ‖ *1–2 tablespoons icing sugar*

ONE Put the sweetcorn kernels in a blender or food processor and blend until smooth. Add all the remaining ingredients, except the icing sugar, and process until well mixed. **TWO** Pour the mixture into a well-greased 20 cm (8 inch) diameter cake tin and bake in a preheated oven, 160°C (325°F), Gas Mark 3, for about 35 minutes, or until a wooden cocktail stick inserted into the centre comes out clean. **THREE** Remove from the oven and leave to rest for 10 minutes. Run the tip of a pointed knife around the edge of the tin to loosen the cake and invert on to a plate. Sift the icing sugar on top. Serve warm.

Serves 6

NUTRIENT ANALYSIS PER SERVING 1236 kJ – 294 kcal – 7 g protein – 38 g carbohydrate – 17 g sugars – 14 g fat – 7 g saturates – 3 g fibre – 454 mg sodium

HEALTHY TIP Sweetcorn contains beta-carotene, small amounts of B vitamins and vitamins A and C. It is also a useful source of protein and rich in fibre.

Raspberry sorbet

Known in Mexico as *nieves*, sorbets are a traditional frozen dessert made with water, sugar and fresh fruit. Raspberries are harvested during all the warmer months of the year; depending on the region, they are available from May through to November.

INGREDIENTS *400 g (13 oz) fresh raspberries* ‖ *150 g (5 oz) granulated sugar* ‖ *500 ml (17 fl oz) water* ‖ *freshly squeezed juice of ½ lime, or to taste* ‖ *mint sprigs, to decorate*

ONE Put the raspberries in a blender or food processor and blend to a purée. Pass through a sieve and set aside. **TWO** Put the sugar in a heavy-based saucepan, add the measured water and heat over a low heat, stirring constantly, until the sugar has completely dissolved. Increase the heat, bring to the boil and gently boil for 5 minutes. Remove from the heat and add the raspberry purée and lime juice. **THREE** Freeze the raspberry mixture in an ice cream maker according to the manufacturer's instructions. Alternatively, pour into a shallow, freezerproof container and freeze for about 1 hour until beginning to solidify. Return to the blender or the food processor and blend to break up the ice crystals. Return to the container and freeze again for 3–4 hours until firm. **FOUR** Serve in scoops, decorated with mint sprigs.

Serves 4

NUTRIENT ANALYSIS PER SERVING 740 kJ – 173 kcal – 1 g protein – 44 g carbohydrate – 44 g sugars – 0 g fat – 00 g saturates – 7 g fibre – 0 mg sodium

HEALTHY TIP Raspberries are an excellent source of calcium, magnesium, phosphorus, potassium and vitamins B3 and C. They also are an effective antioxidant and astringent.

Mango sorbet

Fruit sorbets are very popular throughout the country and different regions have developed their own varieties according to the season and the local fruits. In the state of Veracruz, mango sorbet is one of the most popular flavours sold by street vendors.

INGREDIENTS *5–6 ripe mangoes* ‖ *3 tablespoons granulated sugar, or to taste* ‖ *3 tablespoons water* ‖ *a few drops of freshly squeezed lime juice, or to taste* ‖ *mint sprigs, to decorate (optional)*

ONE Peel the mangoes, remove the flesh and put in a blender or food processor with the sugar, measured water and lime juice. Blend until smooth. Taste and add more sugar or lime juice as necessary. **TWO** Freeze the mango mixture in an ice cream maker according to the manufacturer's instructions. Alternatively, pour into a shallow, freezerproof container and freeze for about 1 hour until beginning to solidify. Return to the blender or food processor and blend to break up the ice crystals. Return to the container and freeze again for 3–4 hours until firm. **THREE** Serve in scoops, decorated with mint sprigs, if liked.

Serves 4

NUTRIENT ANALYSIS PER SERVING 710 kJ – 166 kcal – 1 g protein – 42 g carbohydrate – 42 g sugars – 0 g fat – 0 g saturates – 5 g fibre – 4 mg sodium

HEALTHY TIP In addition to their exquisite and delicate taste, mangoes are an excellent source of vitamins A and C.

Margarita tequila cocktail

The famed Mexican cocktail Margarita is very popular in bars and restaurants all over the country. Combining tequila, lime juice, sugar syrup and orange-flavoured liqueur, it is traditionally served in a glass that has had its rim dipped in lime juice and then coated with salt.

INGREDIENTS *400 g (13 oz) ice cubes* ‖ *125 ml (4 fl oz) white tequila* ‖ *125 ml (4 fl oz) Cointreau* ‖ *125 ml (4 fl oz) freshly squeezed lime juice* ‖ *60 ml (2½ fl oz) sugar syrup*

TO SERVE *lime wedges, for preparing the glasses and to decorate* ‖ *salt, for preparing the glasses*

ONE Rub the rims of 4 Martini glasses with a lime wedge, then dip lightly into a dish of salt. **TWO** Place the ice cubes in a blender, add the tequila, Cointreau, lime juice and sugar syrup and blend at high speed for 30 seconds. **THREE** Pour the tequila mixture into the prepared glasses, decorate with lime wedges and serve immediately.

Serves 4

NUTRIENT ANALYSIS PER SERVING 825 kJ – 200 kcal – 0 g protein – 16 g carbohydrate – 16 g sugars – 0 g fat – 0 g saturates – 0 g fibre – 0 mg sodium

HEALTHY TIP As with all alcoholic beverages, this cocktail must be consumed in moderation. However, the vitamin C from the lime can be helpful in protecting the body from some of the harmful effects of the alcohol. If you are concerned about your salt intake, omit the salt on the glass rim.

Hibiscus water

Hibiscus flowers, with their acid flavours and bright red colour, are widely used in Mexico. This refreshing drink made with the dried flowers is one of the most popular beverages all over the country. Dried hibiscus flowers are available from some delicatessens as well as specialist Mexican food suppliers.

INGREDIENTS *100 g (3½ oz) dried hibiscus flowers* ‖ *1.5 litres (2½ pints) water* ‖ *50 g (2 oz) caster sugar, or to taste* ‖ *ice cubes to serve*

ONE Put the hibiscus flowers and 1 litre (1¾ pints) of the measured water in a large saucepan over a medium heat and bring to the boil. Reduce the heat and simmer for about 8 minutes. Remove from the heat and leave to infuse for 10–15 minutes. **TWO** Strain the infusion into a jug. Add the sugar and the remaining water. Stir thoroughly and leave to cool. Cover and chill in the refrigerator until required. **THREE** Serve with ice cubes.

Serves 4

NUTRIENT ANALYSIS PER SERVING 273 kJ – 64 kcal – 0 g protein – 15 g carbohydrate – 13 g sugars – 0 g fat – 0 g saturates – 0 g fibre – 0 mg sodium

HEALTHY TIP Hibiscus contains antioxidants that help control cholesterol levels and reduce heart disease. Studies have demonstrated that hibiscus flowers have a diuretic property and also mild blood vessel-dilating effects.

Melon water

In local markets all over the country you can often see stalls displaying large jars full of refreshing and delicious fruit coolers. The seeds of the melon are used to make this refreshing drink – ideal for quenching your thirst on a hot summer's day.

INGREDIENTS *1 ripe cantaloupe melon* ‖ *1 litre (1¾ pints) water* ‖ *50 g (2 oz) caster sugar, or to taste* ‖ *ice cubes, to serve*

ONE Peel the melon. Roughly chop 500 g (1 lb) of the melon flesh, put in blender with the seeds and blend to a purée. Add some of the measured water. **TWO** Strain the melon mixture into a jug. Add the sugar and the remaining water and stir thoroughly. Cover and chill in the refrigerator until required. **THREE** To serve, pour the chilled melon water into 4 glasses, add some ice and decorate with a few small cubes of melon, if desired.

Serves 4

NUTRIENT ANALYSIS PER SERVING 310 kJ – 73 kcal – 0 g protein – 18 g carbohydrate – 18 g sugars – 0 g fat – 0 g saturates – 0 g fibre – 0 mg sodium

HEALTHY TIP Cantaloupe melons are not only sweet and refreshing, they are also highly nutritious. They are good source of potassium and vitamins A and C. They are also an excellent cleanser and rehydrator.

Christmas hot punch

This is the most popular drink served in Mexico during the Christmas and New Year festivities, prepared with seasonal fruits cooked in water with cinnamon and raw sugar. Adults drink the punch with *piquete*, which means that it is laced with alcohol. Sugar cane stalks are available from West Indian food shops.

INGREDIENTS *2.5 litres (4 pints) water* ‖ *8 pitted prunes* ‖ *10 organic dried apricots, quartered* ‖ *3 guavas, quartered* ‖ *100 g (3½ oz) sugar cane stalks, peeled and cut into strips* ‖ *50 g (2 oz) dried hibiscus flowers* ‖ *1 apple, cored and cut into 8 segments* ‖ *1 tablespoon raisins* ‖ *1–2 cinnamon sticks* ‖ *75 g (3 oz) caster sugar, or to taste* ‖ *125 ml (4 fl oz) dark rum, or to taste*

ONE Bring the measured water to the boil in a large saucepan over a high heat. Add the prunes and apricots, reduce the heat and simmer for 5 minutes. Add the guavas, sugar cane, hibiscus, apple, raisins, cinnamon sticks and sugar and simmer over a low heat for 30 minutes, stirring occasionally. Taste the punch and add a little more sugar if necessary. Stir well. **TWO** Remove from the heat, add the rum and stir well. **THREE** Ladle into individual mugs and serve immediately.

Serves 6–8

NUTRIENT ANALYSIS PER SERVING 690 kJ – 163 kcal – 1 g protein – 30 g carbohydrate – 30 g sugars – 0 g fat – 0 g saturates – 6 g fibre – 13 mg sodium

HEALTHY TIP This punch contains several healthy fruits. The guava is an outstanding source of vitamin C and soluble fibre, while the raisins, prunes and apricots all have valuable antioxidant effects in the inhibiting and controlling of the harmful action of free radicals.

Michelada iced spicy beer

Beer is perhaps the most popular alcoholic beverage in Mexico. It goes very well with Mexican dishes, so it is widely found in restaurants all over the country. It should be served cold or very cold. In some places where the weather is very hot, *michelada* is the favourite choice.

INGREDIENTS *125 g (4 oz) ice cubes* ‖ *25 ml (1 fl oz) freshly squeezed lime juice* ‖ *a few drops of Worcestershire sauce* ‖ *2 drops of Tabasco sauce* ‖ *375 ml (13 fl oz) bottle Mexican beer, chilled*

TO SERVE *lime wedges, for preparing the glass and to decorate* ‖ *salt, for preparing the glass*

ONE Rub the rim of the glass with a lime wedge, then dip lightly into a dish of salt. **TWO** Place the ice cubes in the glass and add the lime juice and Worcestershire and Tabasco sauces. Pour in the chilled beer. Decorate with a lime wedge and serve immediately.

Serves 1

NUTRIENT ANALYSIS PER SERVING 468 kJ – 114 kcal – 1 g protein – 7 g carbohydrate – 7 g sugars – 0 g fat – 0 g saturates – 0 g fibre – 50 mg sodium

HEALTHY TIP Beer is relatively low in alcohol. Nevertheless, it must be consumed in moderation. If you are concerned about your salt intake, omit the salt on the glass rim.

Red grapefruit water

Fresh citrus beverages are commonly served in most Mexicans homes at lunchtime. This combination of red or pink grapefruit and oranges is highly refreshing and is becoming very popular. You can also add some tangerine juice, when in season.

INGREDIENTS *1 red or pink grapefruit* ‖ *2 oranges* ‖ *2–3 tablespoons caster sugar* ‖ *ice cubes, to serve*

ONE Squeeze the juice from the grapefruit and the oranges. Pour into a jug and add enough water to make 1 litre (1¾ pints). Add the sugar to taste and stir thoroughly. **TWO** Cover and chill in the refrigerator until required. Serve with ice cubes.

Serves 4

NUTRIENT ANALYSIS PER SERVING 427 kJ – 100 kcal – 1 g protein – 26 g carbohydrate – 26 g sugars – 0 g fat – 0 g saturates – 0 g fibre – 6 mg sodium

HEALTHY TIP This citrus drink is rich in vitamin C and also contains vitamin A, calcium, phosphorus, magnesium, copper, potassium and folic acid. It is excellent for the cardiovascular system, and beneficial for colds, flu and sore throats.

Sangrita tequila chaser

Whenever you ask for tequila in bars and restaurants in Mexico, it will usually be served accompanied with a *sangrita* (little blood). Each restaurant has its own recipe, but this sweet and spicy, red beverage is typically a blended mixture of tomato, orange and lime juice and is seasoned with salt and chilli.

INGREDIENTS *250 ml (8 fl oz) tomato juice* ‖ *60 ml (2½ fl oz) freshly squeezed orange juice* ‖ *30 ml (1 fl oz) freshly squeezed lime juice* ‖ *1 tablespoon finely chopped onion* ‖ *1 teaspoon finely chopped green chilli (deseeded for a milder taste)* ‖ *salt and freshly ground black pepper* ‖ *tequila, to serve*

ONE Place all the ingredients in a blender and blend to purée. Check the seasoning. Cover and chill in the refrigerator until required. **TWO** Serve chilled with a shot of your favourite tequila.

Serves 4

NUTRIENT ANALYSIS PER SERVING 69 kJ – 16 kcal – 1 g protein – 4 g carbohydrate – 3 g sugars – 0 g fat – 0 g saturates – 0 g fibre – 144 mg sodium

HEALTHY TIP The healthy tomato juice is enriched with the nutrients from the orange and lime juice, making this drink a potent antiseptic beverage.

Rice and almond horchata

Horchata is a popular refreshing drink in Mexico, made by steeping nuts or grains. It is an ancient drink prepared in many places in the Mediterranean region, and was introduced to Mexico by the Spanish. This version from the state of Oaxaca is made with ground rice and almonds spiced with cinnamon and sweetened with sugar. It is generally served cold with ice cubes.

INGREDIENTS *250 g (8 oz) long-grain white rice* ‖ *750 ml (1¼ pints) water* ‖ *1 cinnamon stick* ‖ *500 ml (17 fl oz) semi-skimmed milk* ‖ *100 g (3½ oz) ground almonds* ‖ *85 g (3¼ oz) caster sugar, or to taste*
TO SERVE *ice cubes* ‖ *ground cinnamon*

ONE Rinse the rice briefly to remove any impurities and drain. Soak in 500 ml (17 fl oz) of the measured water in a bowl. **TWO** Heat a small, dry frying pan over a medium heat. Crumble in the cinnamon stick and lightly toast for a few seconds. Add to the rice and leave to stand overnight. **THREE** Transfer the rice mixture to a blender and blend until smooth. Pass through a sieve, then add the remaining water, milk, ground almonds and sugar. Stir thoroughly. **FOUR** Transfer the mixture to a jug, cover and chill in the refrigerator until required. **FIVE** Just before serving, stir thoroughly, pour into a glass with ice cubes and dust the top with cinnamon.

Serves 4–6

NUTRIENT ANALYSIS PER SERVING 2194 kJ – 520 kcal – 14 g protein – 85 g carbohydrate – 30 g sugars – 17 g fat – 2 g saturates – 5 g fibre – 76 mg sodium

HEALTHY TIP Rice, which is cholesterol- and gluten-free, is low in sodium, contains only a trace of fat and is an excellent source of complex carbohydrates. Almonds are very alkaline and contain calcium, magnesium, potassium and folic acid, as well as vitamins B2, B3 and E. They are a good source of protein and a useful food for those who are underweight.

Strawberry atole

Popular throughout Mexico, *atole* is a pre-Hispanic, very thick beverage consisting of masa harina, water or milk, sweetened with sugar and flavoured with crushed fruit and spices. There are many variants, including different thickening agents, such as the cornflour used in this recipe. It is the traditional accompaniment for *tamales* (steamed corn dumplings) and usually drunk on cold mornings.

INGREDIENTS *400 g (13 oz) fresh strawberries, hulled* ‖ *60 g (2¼ oz) caster sugar, or to taste* ‖ *350 ml (12 fl oz) semi-skimmed milk* ‖ *3 tablespoons cornflour* ‖ *350 ml (12 fl oz) cold water*

ONE Put the strawberries, sugar and milk in a blender and blend until smooth. Set aside. **TWO** Blend the cornflour with some of the measured water to make a smooth paste, then add the remaining water. Bring to the boil in a saucepan, then reduce the heat and simmer for 5–8 minutes, stirring constantly. Gradually add the strawberry mixture and gently simmer for about 10 minutes until the mixture thickens. **THREE** Serve immediately in individual mugs.

Serves 4

NUTRIENT ANALYSIS PER SERVING 649 kJ – 153 kcal – 4 g protein – 33 g carbohydrate – 26 g sugars – 2 g fat – 1 g saturates – 2 g fibre – 58 mg sodium

HEALTHY TIP Strawberries, rich in antioxidant nutrients, are an exceptional source of vitamin C, low in sodium and high in potassium. They also are an excellent source of pectin, the soluble fibre that helps eliminate cholesterol.

Hot chocolate

Cacao is one of the most important Mexican contributions to the gastronomic world. Chocolate is a pre-Hispanic ritual beverage, made with cacao and water, served cold with plenty of foam. The present practice of using milk and serving it hot is widely accepted. One of the most popular chocolate bars used to prepare this drink contains ground cacao, sugar, cinnamon, almond and vanilla.

INGREDIENTS *1 litre (1¾ pints) semi-skimmed milk or water* ‖ *150 g (5 oz) plain dark chocolate, containing at least 55% cocoa solids, chopped*

ONE Heat the milk or water with the chocolate in a saucepan over a medium heat. Bring to the boil and remove the pan from the heat. **TWO** Using a whisk, beat the chocolate mixture vigorously until the chocolate has completely melted and a thick layer of foam has formed over the surface. **THREE** Pour the chocolate into individual cups and serve immediately.

Serves 4

NUTRIENT ANALYSIS PER SERVING 1310 kJ – 312 kcal – 10 g protein – 37 g carbohydrate – 35 g sugars – 15 g fat – 9 g saturates – 0 g fibre – 140 mg sodium

HEALTHY TIP In spite of their fat content, cocoa beans are rather nutritious; they supply useful amounts of proteins, some B vitamins and trace elements, particularly iron and magnesium. Chocolate can give a short-lived boost of energy because of its sugar content. It should be drunk in moderation.

Index

Acknowledgements

EXECUTIVE EDITOR Nicky Hill

PROJECT EDITORS Leanne Bryan and Ruth Hamilton

DEPUTY CREATIVE DIRECTOR Karen Sawyer

DESIGNER Janis Utton

SENIOR PRODUCTION CONTROLLER Manjit Sihra

PHOTOGRAPHY Emma Neish / © Octopus Publishing Group Ltd

FOOD STYLIST Sunil Vijayakar

PROPS STYLIST Liz Hippisley

Picture acknowledgements

Special Photography: © **Octopus Publishing Group Limited**/Emma Neish